D1488278

FERGUSON
CAREER BIOGRAPHIES

ROBERTO
CLEMENTE

Baseball Player

Jerry Roberts

Ferguson
An imprint of ☑®Facts On File

Roberto Clemente: Baseball Player

Ferguson
An imprint of Facts On File, Inc.
132 West 31st Street
New York NY 10001

Library of Congress Cataloging-in-Publication Data

Roberts, Jerry
  Roberto Clemente : baseball player / Jerry Roberts
      p. cm.
  Includes index.
  ISBN 0-8160-6072-X (hc : alk. paper)
  1. Clemente, Roberto, 1934–1972—Juvenile literature. 2. Baseball players—Puerto Rico—Biography—Juvenile literature. I. Title.
  GV865.C45R63 2006
  796.357'092—dc22   2005006439

Ferguson books are available at special discounts when purchased in bulk quantities for businesses, associations, institutions, or sales promotions. Please call our Special Sales Department in New York at (212) 967-8800 or (800) 322-8755.

You can find Ferguson on the World Wide Web at http://www.fergpubco.com

Text design by David Strelecky

Pages 94–110 adapted from Ferguson's *Encyclopedia of Careers and Vocational Guidance, Thirteenth Edition*

Printed in the United States of America

MP JT 10 9 8 7 6 5 4 3 2 1

This book is printed on acid-free paper.

CONTENTS

1

CHAMPION, RECORD-SETTER, AND HERO

Anytime you have the opportunity to accomplish something for somebody who comes behind you and you don't do it, you are wasting your time on this Earth.

—Roberto Clemente

Roberto Clemente came to the public's attention in the final years of his life in three big ways. These big moments came after years of underappreciation, even though Roberto was the best hitter and perhaps the best all-around baseball player of the 1960s. Two of these moments ensured Roberto—the Pittsburgh Pirates' greatest all-time player—a lofty place in the Baseball Hall of Fame, where he was the first Latino player ever enshrined. The third moment, although one of great tragedy, captured forever his uncommon courage and respect for humanity.

Through his outstanding life and career, Roberto Clemente became an inspiration for people around the world. (MLB Photos via Getty Images)

In 2003, 30 years after Roberto suddenly departed the world, President George W. Bush posthumously presented him with the nation's highest civilian award, the Presidential Medal of Freedom. Accepted by Roberto's widow, Vera Clemente, this honor renewed Roberto's memory in the public's mind. He had gone beyond his role as a significant figure in American sports: He had become an icon of both the Latino and African-American cultures and a source of inspiration to people around the world.

"Jackie Robinson of the Latin"

Felipe Alou, manager of the Montreal Expos and San Francisco Giants, said that Roberto was "the Jackie Robinson of the Latin. . . . He was the one who rose to the occasion." Alou was referring to a lifetime of occasions through which Roberto paved the way for Latin ballplayers in America.

Roberto's impact on baseball is still felt today. Each year, Major League Baseball cites a player "who has excelled in a comeback or has greatly helped the community" with the annual Roberto Clemente Award, whose recipients have included Willie Mays, Rod Carew, Cal Ripken Jr., Kirby Puckett, Sammy Sosa, and Tony Gwynn. (In fact, the Chicago Cubs' Sosa wears No. 21—the same number as Roberto—to commemorate his boyhood hero.)

But Roberto is not just celebrated in the baseball community. All around the nation, in Chicago, Philadelphia, New York, and elsewhere, there are schools and parks named after this hero who meant so much to so many.

World Series Hero

In his first big moment of international fame, Roberto dominated a seven-game World Series the way few players ever have. In 1971 he led the Pittsburgh Pirates to the world championship through skill, leadership, competitiveness, and enormous pride.

By watching Roberto play baseball, fans everywhere were exposed to a playing style they had never seen before. Sportswriter Roger Angell described Roberto's playing as "running and throwing and hitting at something close to the level of absolute perfection, playing to win, but also playing as if it were a form of punishment for everyone else on the field."

Hammering out hits and unleashing awesome throws, Roberto always gave a majestic performance. "He didn't just play right field," said Hall of Famer Frank Robinson, who played against Clemente in the '71 series. "He performed out there—whirl and throw to third base, not turn and throw, like most of us. He would whirl like a ballet dancer. Even though you were playing against him, you started to watch to see what he would do next. 'Did you see that? Did that happen? Did he really do that?' And you'd say, 'Yes, he did.' Wow!"

Even Roberto's own teammates, who understood him as both a friend and great player, were stunned. "He said, 'If you guys get me to the World Series, I'll win it,'" said Willie Stargell, who led the league that year with 48 home runs. "It was almost like, 'You guys sit down. I've got a job to do. I'll show you how it's done.'"

Roberto's two-out home run in the fourth inning of the deciding seventh game gave the Pirates their 2-1 win. In the heat of that series Roberto said, "I want to be remembered as a ballplayer who gave all he had to give."

Although this was Roberto's second World Series win with the Pirates (the first was in 1960), in 1971 he definitely led the show. An international television audience finally saw what Pittsburgh fans had seen from "the Great One" for nearly two decades.

During all of his time on the field, Roberto never forgot that he was a role model for fans everywhere. "It was like he had to make sure all of the Latin American countries were represented through himself," Stargell said. "And he wanted to display his talents, his abilities, his true love of the game. And, believe me, that was his true moment of glory."

Pride in Family and Home

After the 1971 World Series victory, Roberto's first public words were thanks for the blessings of his mother, father, and grandparents on his native island of Puerto Rico. Roberto never wavered in his dedication to his family, to his home island, and to Latin Americans in general. He was always proud of who he was, where he came from, and what he could do on a baseball field. "When I put on my uniform," he said, "I feel I am the proudest man on Earth."

Even though his pride caused others to label him as arrogant early in his career, it made him incredibly competitive, a trait that all great athletes must have. When sportswriters compared him to Willie Mays, Roberto said, "Nonetheless, I play like Roberto Clemente."

3,000th Career Hit

A year after the 1971 World Series, Roberto made international news for the second time.

Roberto was no stranger to honors and awards. He already had to his credit four National League batting titles, four years of 200-plus hits, 12 straight Gold Glove awards, and 14 All-Star Game appearances. He was also the Major League leader of the 1960s in hits (1,877) and average (.328), and he had won Most Valuable Player awards for the National League (1966) and for the 1971 World Series.

But Roberto made a new career leap on September 30, 1972, in the season's final regular-season game. He drilled a double off the left-center-field wall at Pittsburgh's Three Rivers Stadium against the New York Mets, and thereby became a member of the 3,000-hit club.

Only 10 previous players, including Hall of Famers Ty Cobb and Honus Wagner, had collected as many hits in their careers. At the time, Willie Mays and Henry Aaron—the two players Clemente was most often compared to—had achieved the feat a few years prior to Roberto.

Mission of Mercy

Just months after his 3,000th hit, Roberto again captured the attention of the world—this time through tragedy. In December of 1972 more than 10,000 people died in a catastrophic earthquake in Managua, Nicaragua. It registered 5.6 on the Richter scale. Each day throughout the holidays, international emergency units scrambled to pull hundreds of survivors and the dead out of the rubble.

Roberto had visited Nicaragua earlier that year on a barnstorming tour and became friendly with the locals. Hearing that people were stealing relief supplies destined for the devastated nation, Roberto volunteered to organize relief efforts on behalf of his native island of Puerto Rico. He went on Puerto Rican TV to make a personal pitch for food and donations. To guarantee that the food, clothing, and other necessities reached the victims, he decided to deliver the goods himself.

At the time, by his own estimation, Roberto had at least five or six years left to play in the big leagues. His physique and exacting hitting eye were still in premium condition, as was his batting average. But sadly, Roberto would never finish out his historic career.

On December 31, 1972, Roberto kissed his wife, Vera, good-bye. His son, seven-year-old Roberto Jr., tearfully protested three times that the airplane loaded with the supplies was going to crash. "I cried for a while," Roberto Jr. remembered decades later. "He came outside and gave me a hug and a kiss. And that was it."

Roberto and four others boarded a four-propeller DC-7 loaded with supplies for the quake victims. The plane took off from San Juan Airport at 9:22 P.M. bound for Managua for the third time that week. The first explosion sounded as the plane cleared palm trees near the shore after takeoff. The fourth explosion, according to a witness, resounded before the plane tilted nose-down into the ocean a mile from land. There were no survivors. Only the body of pilot Jerry Hill was found.

Pirates Star Mourned

The next morning the world reacted with shock and disbelief. Clemente's friend and teammate Manny Sanguillen joined thousands of mourners shoulder-to-shoulder on the shore of the Atlantic Ocean on New Year's Day.

Governor Luis A. Ferre declared three days of official mourning in Puerto Rico. On January 2 President Richard M. Nixon called Clemente "one of the greatest baseball players of our time." The president also said, "In the tragedy of his untimely death, we are reminded that he deserved even greater respect and admiration for his splendid qualities as a generous and kind human being."

Roberto's baseball accomplishments were more than enough to earn him a place in the Baseball Hall of Fame in Cooperstown, New York. But his story is much more than that of a great baseball player. It is the story of a pioneer of the Latin-American legacy in the United States, and a passionate advocate of people of color everywhere. It is a story that starts on the island of Puerto Rico, with a little boy who loved baseball from the very beginning.

2

BARRIO BOYHOOD AND BASEBALL DREAMS

While I was a little kid, I wanted to be a baseball player. . . . The more I think about it, God wanted me to play baseball.

—Roberto Clemente

Melchor Clemente had grown up in Puerto Rico under Spanish rule and was 17 when it was ceded to the United States after the Spanish-American War in 1898. He was the father of five children and stepfather of two more. He worked as the horse-mounted foreman of a sugar-cane-chopping crew in Carolina, Puerto Rico. In his day, men with machetes harvested even the great modern plantations.

Melchor was married to Luisa Walker de Clemente, who had been a widow. The family lived in a five-bedroom wood house in San Anton, a middle- and lower-class neighborhood of Carolina. The home contained a luxury in rural Puerto Rico: an indoor bathroom. Melchor, who also became a general contractor, and Luisa eventually outlived four of their children including the youngest, Roberto, who was nicknamed "Momen" by his sister.

Roberto Clemente Walker was born August 18, 1934. As a young kid, he loved to bounce and catch a rubber ball off the ceiling and floors, and he joined his brothers— Martino, Lorenzo, and Andres—in San Anton for ball-games. He was eight when he started playing in neighborhood games, where the other players were at least 10 or older.

"He had the combative fury of very few athletes," remembered Manuel Maldonado Denis, a childhood friend. "All you had to do was look at Momen to know that he had been born to play baseball." People would remark about his enormous hands, which were evident even in childhood. Roberto loved baseball so much that he used to sleep with a baseball that he caught after it had blown out of San Juan's Sixto Escobar Stadium.

Roberto's first bat was a guava tree branch. His glove was made from a coffee bean sack. He often recalled how his mother tried to burn one of his first actual baseball bats because he would forget to come home from the ball field for meals. "But I got it out of the fire and saved it," he said.

Solid Family Foundation

The Great Depression that ravaged the United States during the 1930s also extended to the U.S. island colony of Puerto Rico (which means "rich port"). Puerto Rico became a U.S. commonwealth in 1952.

"When I was a boy, I realized what lovely persons my father and mother were," Roberto said. "I was treated real good. I learned the right way to live. I never heard any hate in my house. Not for anybody. I never heard my mother say a bad word to my father, or my father to my mother. During the war, when food all over Puerto Rico was limited, we never went hungry. They always found a way to feed us. We kids were first, and they were second."

The young Roberto grew into his teens during World War II, admiring the ballplayers he saw in Sixto Escobar Stadium. Roberto's favorite player was Monte Irvin, a shortstop who became one of the first African-American stars in the National League—for the New York Giants—after Jackie Robinson broke the color barrier in 1947. (Irvin eventually became a representative for the baseball commissioner's office in 1968 and was enshrined in the Hall of Fame in 1973, the same year as Clemente.)

"I first met Roberto Clemente in the early '40s in Puerto Rico," Irvin said. "I used to play down there. And this was [when I was] in the Negro Leagues. He was just a youngster. One day I let him carry my bag in order [for him] to get into the stadium. So, we became friendly. I used to give him a ball. I . . . might have given him a glove that I had. But I never did see him play."

Roberto began playing organized ball in 1948 at age 14 as a shortstop for Sello Rojo, a Carolina tournament softball team sponsored by a rice company. One day a rice wholesaler named Roberto Marin was driving through San Anton when he saw kids batting tomato sauce cans with sticks. One kid "hit those cans pretty far," Marin remembered. He signed Roberto, who had always played with older kids, to play on his team. But now Roberto was playing with grown men, traveling with the team to San Juan.

Amateur and Early Pro Years

Three years later, at Julio C. Vizarrondo High School, Roberto was both a baseball and track star. "I remember Roberto Clemente in 1951–52," recalled Orlando Cepeda, a fellow Puerto Rican who played for the San Francisco Giants and St. Louis Cardinals. "He used to play amateur ball. Before that, he used to play softball. Everybody used to know who he was. He used to run track, throw the javelin, everything." Everybody also knew about Roberto's competitive edge. "Roberto," Cepeda said, "was never second to anyone.

"He was a shortstop," he said. "My father used to be manager of a team called Juncos, and it was the No. 1 team in Puerto Rico. Used to be like the Yankees. Everybody wanted to play for Juncos then, the best players on the whole island. So, we have a guy at shortstop who was so established. He say, 'Don't sign him [Clemente].' So . . . two years later . . . [Roberto] signed for Santurce."

Indeed, Clemente signed for a $400 bonus and a $40-a-week salary with the Santurce Cangrejeros, or "Crabbers." He initially sat the bench as a backup player during the 1952–53 season and hated it. One night, playing against Caguas, he was used as a pinch hitter with the bases loaded. He clubbed a diamond-clearing double to right field. From then on, he started.

The following year Roberto played left field for Santurce. In center for the Crabbers that Winter League season was Willie Mays, who would win the National League batting crown in 1954 with a .345 average playing on the New York Giants. The experience had a big impact on Roberto.

"They got along very well together, a young boy with a young star," Roberto Marin recalled. "Mays was a very good guy. When there was a grounder to the outfield,

In Puerto Rico, Roberto played for the Santurce Cangrejeros.
(National Baseball Library, Cooperstown, N.Y.)

Mays would remind him, show him how one outfielder backs up another. I think it was the inspiration of playing next to a star like Mays, and doing a good job, that was most important. Anyway, that year Roberto became a first-class ballplayer. From then on, he went up and up."

Dodgers Contract

By this time Major League scouts were already becoming aware of Roberto's potential. In a joint tryout in 1952 organized by the Crabbers and the Brooklyn Dodgers, scout Al Campanis asked one of the 72 hopefuls to duplicate a throw Roberto had just made to home plate from the furthest reaches of center field. Roberto obliged and again hurled a 350-foot strike.

"How could I miss him?" Campanis asked years later. "He was the greatest natural athlete I have ever seen as a free agent." Roberto ran 60 yards in 6.4 seconds—twice. Campanis made mental notes about the high school senior. At this time Major League teams were finally starting to look for talent in the islands and in Central and South America. Signing with big-league clubs were Minnie Minoso, Bobby Avila, Vic Power, Camilo Pascual, Felipe Alou, Sandy Amoros, and others. Nine teams approached Roberto in 1953, including the Giants.

The Milwaukee Braves supposedly offered Roberto a $28,000 signing bonus. But by then he had already committed to the Brooklyn Dodgers' offer of a $10,000 signing bonus and $5,000 salary. In 1954 he would play on the Dodgers' International League farm team, the Montreal Royals. The Dodgers were mainly interested in keeping Clemente from signing with the Giants, because they would then have to face their New York rival with Mays and Clemente in the same outfield. But as Roberto would later discover, the Dodgers also had other reasons for keeping him in Montreal as opposed to the team's Major League club in Brooklyn.

On February 19, 1954, Roberto and his father co-signed a telegram to the Dodgers accepting the offer. The 74-year-old Melchor Clemente had two pieces of advice at San Juan Airport for his 19-year-old son, whose understanding of English was evolving from high school dabbling. "Buy yourself a good car," Melchor said, "and don't depend on anybody."

"Hidden" in Montreal

Although so many others would come to depend on Roberto, upon his arrival in Montreal he needed to depend on a few people himself. One was Tommy Lasorda, a pitcher whose big-league record would conclude at 0-4 after three seasons and who went on to become manager of the Los Angeles Dodgers. "I had to take care of him, because he couldn't speak one word of English," Lasorda remembered. Because of Roberto's heavily accented English, "He couldn't go get anything to eat, so he would wait for me in the morning, until I woke up. And then when I would come down to the lobby, he was sitting there, waiting for me. And he was hungry."

Roberto's extreme talent was so evident that the Dodgers knew they could not play the young Puerto Rican every day. "He wanted to play bad," Lasorda recalled. "He was disappointed that he wasn't playing more." Pittsburgh Pirates scout Howie Haak, who was ordered to shadow Clemente in Montreal, remembered that the youngster only went to bat four times from August until the end of the playoffs. Frustrated with his lack of time on the field, Clemente left the dugout during pregame warm-ups and went back to his hotel to pack and go back to Puerto Rico. This was one of the first incidents that gave Roberto a reputation for feisty behavior.

"I went down to the hotel," Haak remembered. "[Roberto] didn't speak English too good and I didn't speak anything of Spanish, but I said, 'Come back to the ball-park. If you want to play in the Major Leagues, you better come back to the ballpark with me.' By the time he got dressed, they were ready to start the game." Roberto didn't realize it at the time, but he had been a pawn in a racial battle.

Racial Complexities

Jackie Robinson, the first player to break the color line by playing Major League Baseball, was adamant when he said that an obviously talented black player should not be sitting on the Brooklyn Dodgers bench. He said this in light of an unofficial quota rule that the Dodgers had imposed. The quota came about after Sandy Amoros became the fifth African American on the Dodgers roster following the 1953 season, joining Robinson, Roy Campanella, Don Newcombe, and Junior Gilliam.

Jackie Robinson was the first player to break the color line in Major League Baseball. (Associated Press)

In the racially segregated United States of the 1950s, some people were alarmed that, for the first time ever, black players could potentially outnumber white players on the field five to four. In an effort to prevent public outcry, the Dodgers decided to keep a maximum of three players of color on the field at one time, regardless of those players' talents. The Dodgers' official excuse for "hiding" Roberto in Montreal was that its starting outfield already was composed of three .300 hitters: Robinson, Duke Snider, and Carl Furillo. The real reason was more complex: It was a combination of the era's atmosphere of racism (seen in the quota) and a short-lived rule of baseball. This other rule said that any player whose signing bonus was more than $4,000 could be drafted by any other team if he was not on the signing team's Major League roster at the season's close. Since Roberto had received a $10,000 signing bonus from the Dodgers and was not on their Major League roster because of the racial quota, he was a prime pick for the draft, despite the organization's best efforts to "hide" the valuable player in Montreal.

Welcome to Pittsburgh

In 1954 the last-place Pittsburgh Pirates had the first selection in the draft. They chose Clemente. He would have a new beginning in Pittsburgh, where the team was so used to losing that it had almost become the Pirates' defining trait. However, Clemente's arrival in training camp in 1955 helped to change the team's losing mentality.

"The guy had so much talent," Pirates pitcher Bob Friend recalled. "You could see it, you know. And, really, for a first-year man, he had a lot of confidence, too."

Dick Groat, Pittsburgh's shortstop, was amazed. Decades later he remarked, "I've always said, after playing with Bobby from 1955 to '62, Bobby Clemente was the greatest God-given talent I've ever seen on a baseball diamond. There wasn't anything he couldn't do as well if not better than anyone that I have ever seen."

3

MAJOR LEAGUE GROWING PAINS

I'm Puerto Rican, I'm black, and I am between the walls.

—Roberto Clemente

Pittsburgh in 1955 was the hub of the coal and steel industries. It was a big union town, headquarters for many of the nation's large corporations and a home of research and scholarship. The barging of coked coal on its rivers made Pittsburgh one of the busiest ports in the world, even though it was a landlocked city. The steep cobblestone streets wended through ethnically distinct neighborhoods, and the surrounding county, Allegheny, contained more bridges than any other place on Earth.

Many years later, in 1979, Pittsburgh would become "The City of Champions" when the Pirates won the World

Series and the Steelers captured the Super Bowl. But when Roberto Clemente came to town, the teams were truly the pits. The Steelers and the Pirates were among the last-place teams in pro sports. In fact, the Pirates lost 101 games in 1954, putting them dead last in the eight-team National League.

The Pirates general manager, Branch Rickey, had been the general manager of the Brooklyn Dodgers a few years before. In fact, Rickey had engineered the breaking of the Major League's color barrier by signing Jackie Robinson.

Before Roberto Clemente ever made it to Pittsburgh, he faced barriers that he had not known before. He was unprepared for continental American life, especially in the small-town South during spring training. Roberto was used to the Puerto Rican version of America, where racism was rarely overt. But as he soon learned firsthand, racism in the southern United States in the 1950s was a constant reality.

Dealing with Racism

In many ways, racism was a foreign concept to Roberto when he arrived in the United States. "My mother and father never told me to hate anyone, or told me to dislike anyone because of race or color," Clemente said. "As a matter of fact, I started listening to this stuff when I came to the United States." During spring training in the 1950s at Fort Myers, Florida, Roberto and the African-American players, such as Curt Roberts and Bennie Daniels had to stay and eat at the rooming house known as Mr. Earl's in the "colored section" of town.

Meanwhile, the white players and management stayed at a hotel. They traveled in the team bus to away games, while the players of color had to ride in separate cars. They had to drink at different water fountains. They couldn't eat on the road with the team. Mostly, they ate in cars or at picnic tables near the back doors of diners. "We had to bring sandwiches to the black players," remembered Joe L. Brown, Rickey's replacement as general manager in 1956.

"I don't care one way or the other," Clemente once said. "If I am good enough to play here, I have to be good enough to be treated like the rest of the players." Although this demand was only fair, Roberto was seen by some from the get-go as an arrogant and temperamental player.

But he was the proverbial fish out of water in several ways. First, he was younger than practically anyone else in an era when spending five years in the minor leagues was the common rite of passage. "People forget he was 20 years old when he came to the Major Leagues," recalled former Pirates pitcher and broadcaster Nellie King.

Secondly, he was unprepared for racial prejudice. "Roberto Clemente as a Latin American had to deal with as many or more problems than Jackie Robinson did," King said. "Jackie Robinson had to deal with one problem—he was a black American. He understood the prejudices in this country. Clemente came—and he didn't understand."

Finally, although Roberto was slowly expanding his knowledge of English, sportswriters portrayed Roberto's accent in comic ways. "He said, 'I hit the ball,' and they would put that in the paper, 'H-E-E-T,'" said former Pirate Tony Bartirome. Phil Musick, a sportswriter who years later befriended Roberto, recalled, "He was quoted phonetically in the papers. He knew it made him look stupid."

Roberto knew that he often was not understood. Roberto was "a very sensitive individual," Joe L. Brown said, "someone who wasn't comfortable in his surroundings, particularly because, I think, the language. While Roberto spoke English, it was with a much broader accent than he did later on. And I think he was misunderstood."

Although Roberto was sometimes ridiculed on the basis of his youth, color, and manner of speaking, the great African-American talents who followed Jackie Robinson in the big leagues recognized Roberto as a pioneer for Latino and black players.

"It was probably harder on him than it was on me," said Henry Aaron, who joined the Milwaukee Braves in 1954 from the Negro Leagues. "He had to adjust to America; he had to adjust to the language barrier."

Roberto certainly was passionate and proud, but he felt that he needed to raise his voice against racial inequalities so that conditions would be forced to improve.

Brilliant and Different

As the most talented, darkest, and heavily accented player on a white northern team, Roberto was a very visible figure. As such, he was subject to a lot of criticism and media attacks, which led to frustration and defensiveness on his part. Luckily, there was one thing that allowed him to focus and blow off steam during this trying time: playing baseball.

Roberto approached and played baseball differently than most players—a way that most agreed was always brilliant. Roberto quickly became the most unpredictable batter in baseball, able to hit any pitch in any placement anywhere in any park. Pitchers remained as mystified by him in 1972 as they were in 1955, when he singled in his first at-bat, hit .255, and became the Pirates' starting right fielder.

Roberto's at-bats became a baseball ritual. He seemed literally onstage in the batter's box. His slow, deliberate walk from the on-deck circle to batter's box—the club handle gripped in his big hand, elbows bent, head staring downward—played out like the entrance of a much-awaited character in a stage play. "The way he went from the batter's circle to the batter's box was like somebody going to the electric chair," sportswriter Bill Christine remembered.

Roberto would screw the batting helmet down on his head or roll his head from side to side, limbering up his neck. (He was in a San Juan auto accident in 1956 and would continue to have back and neck pain for the remainder of his life.) After the neck swiveling, the excavation started. Roberto would scratch and re-pile the dirt of the batter's box with his cleats until he appeared satisfied. This sometimes took more than a minute.

In his stance he faced slightly forward as he leaned into pitches, the bat pointed straight up. While his bat grip and concentration on the pitcher were always the same, he hit many different ways. He reached to connect the fat part of the bat on outside pitches, but kept his torso over his feet. He dragged his front foot to coil his whole body for powerful line-drive clouts, which was a trademark. He took swings at inside fastballs that could have dinged off his helmet brim to either corkscrew himself into the ground for a strike, or instead leg out a double.

Fielding Prowess

In his second season Roberto proved that he was one of the offensive elite by hitting .311. This placed him third in the league behind batting champ Henry Aaron and Bill Virdon.

"He had a totally different style than anybody," said Pittsburgh pitcher Bob Purkey. "He ran different; he sort of galloped. And, of course, his basket catch was totally different then." Some say Roberto learned the basket catch when he played with Willie Mays that one season in the Puerto Rican Winter League. (Most outfielders caught fly balls above their heads or at least above their sightlines with open upturned gloves. But on easy flies Mays and Roberto would often hold the glove heels close to their torsos and let the ball drop into the leather, creating the appearance of nonchalance.) But Roberto maintained that his basket catch, usually stomach-high, followed by an underhand flip back to the infield, was his own inspiration.

As a defensive right fielder, Roberto had no rival. The other greats of his day agreed. Henry Aaron said, "I don't think anybody played right field better than he did. I mean, he played it the way it should have been played, with grace and elegance."

Roberto often said that he could catch anything in his territory. And right field in Pittsburgh's Forbes Field was the largest territory—in square feet—of any one player's

Roberto was known for his speed and grace on the field.
(Associated Press)

territory in baseball. Forbes Field was the deepest park in the majors: 462 feet to center with the bull pens along the foul lines and an ivy-covered brick wall. Roberto came away from many encounters with that wall wearing ivy vines and needing stitches.

"There was never anybody better at his position than Clemente," said Bill Virdon, who played alongside Roberto in center field for the Pirates for 10 years and later managed Pittsburgh as well as the New York Yankees and

Houston Astros. "He was simply the best in the business, not only because he could catch a ball better than anyone—which he could—or because his arm was so strong, but in every phase of play. He did everything exceptionally well, and then his judgment was better than that. He always threw to the right base.

"He was always where he was supposed to be, backing up, taking balls off the most difficult fences. His arm was powerful, but it was also deadly accurate. Nobody ran on him and when they did run it was from ignorance, not knowledge," Virdon said.

Cannonlike Arm

Roberto's plaque in the Baseball Hall of Fame contains the phrase "rifle-armed defensive star." This is because no player in baseball history is as well-known as Roberto for throwing out runners. Even the fastest players, such as Maury Wills, Lou Brock, and Willie Mays, did not attempt to capture an extra base if they hit the ball to right field when Roberto Clemente was playing.

Roberto's conditioning rituals in both spring training and the off-season primed his bat control and his arm. He would practice bat control by getting friends and neighborhood kids to fling bottle caps toward him from close range. He spent hours throwing baseballs from the right field wall into fruit baskets at second and third bases and home plate. "We were always amazed at that outstanding arm," teammate Bob Friend said. "He used to gun that thing all the way from right field to home plate on the fly."

Clemente and Friend were among the few bright lights on the Pirates in the late 1950s. But in 1958, the year Roberto led outfielders in assists for the first time with 22, the team promoted former infielder Danny Murtaugh to manager. The Pirates, moving from nearly a decade at the bottom of the ranks into a second-place finish, were eight games behind the National League champion Milwaukee Braves. Pitchers Vernon Law, Elroy Face, and Bob Friend improved, and Dick Groat and Bill Mazeroski developed into the premiere double-play combination in baseball.

A trade with Cincinnati brought a couple of influential players into the Pirates organization: third baseman Don Hoak, pitcher Harvey Haddix, and one of the better-hitting catchers of the times, Forrest "Smoky" Burgess. However, the Pirates faltered in 1959 to fourth place as Roberto missed all of that June with an elbow injury after being hit by a pitch. Roberto finished the year hitting .296 and ended his first half-decade in the majors at .281.

"Hothead" Reputation

Roberto had tried, to varying degrees of success, to keep his cool during disagreements with managers Bobby Bragen and Danny Murtaugh. For a while he was infamous for taking out his frustrations on his batting helmets, fueling his reputation as a hothead. As uneasily as he fit into life in Pittsburgh at first, he was critical to the Pirates' success, even though he felt estranged from his teammates.

Roberto had shown that he could be among the league's best hitters. He even set a record: for most triples in a game, with three against the Cincinnati Reds in 1958. He had befriended a Pittsburgh postal worker, "Pittsburgh Phil" Dorsey, who had been Bob Friend's master sergeant in the Army Reserve. Even with Dorsey as his confidante, Roberto, who did not smoke or drink like some of the players, lived a solitary life in Pittsburgh and on the road.

"He didn't understand our ways and we didn't understand his ways," said Bill Mazeroski, a future Hall of Famer who spent 17 years on the Pirates with Clemente. "It was probably the worst time in his career. He probably didn't like us and we didn't like him. I imagine that it was an awfully lonely life in those days."

But Roberto's English improved along with his baseball skills. And the Latin players coming into the majors looked to him for guidance, which he freely gave. He always was willing to mentor younger players, Latino or otherwise, in the ways of hitting and fielding. This would become a regular vocation for Roberto in the coming decade.

4

BLASTING THE BRONX BOMBERS

I love people. I love the minority people. And I love the people who are not big shots. I like common people. I like workers. I like people who have suffered. Because these people, they have a different approach to life than people who really have everything.

—Roberto Clemente

The continuity and prosperity of the 1950s seemed to ease into the next decade without much change. The three television shows, all westerns, that led the ratings in 1959–60—*Gunsmoke, Wagon Train,* and *Have Gun, Will Travel*—were still the top three in 1960–61. The New York Yankees continued to dominate the major leagues with a dynasty led by Mickey Mantle, Whitey Ford, Yogi Berra, and Roger Maris. In the 15 years since World War II, the

Yankees won 8 of the 11 World Series in which they played.

But the 1960s would be a decade of change for the United States in terms of politics, social issues, and even in the world of sports. As sports fans around the nation would witness, the events of the first World Series of the decade proved that the high and mighty could indeed be humbled.

On a clear, chilly October afternoon in 1960, Bill Mazeroski ended three decades of Pittsburgh Pirates medi-

The Pittsburgh Pirates 1960 World Series lineup (Corbis)

ocrity with a ninth-inning, game-winning home run that defeated the Yankees, 10-9, in one of the most exciting seventh games in World Series history. The game marked one of the biggest David vs. Goliath moments in mid-century American sports: The established Yankees were ambushed and defeated by a team of players who were largely working on second starts in their careers or, as in the case of Roberto Clemente, who were just making a name for themselves in America's favorite sport.

Edge Needed to Win

Getting to the pinnacle of a World Series win had not been easy for Roberto or the Pirates, who had not been to the World Series since 1927. To win the National League pennant, the team had to rely on overtaxed pitching, sure-handed defense, and the hitting of Roberto and others who seemed to come through with just enough firepower or glove-reach to win. Roberto took nothing for granted, as his work ethic on the field rated second to none.

The 1960 Pirates needed that edge. The Pirates led the National League in runs (734), hits (1,493), and batting average (.276). They coasted to the pennant, seven games ahead of the Milwaukee Braves and nine in front of the St. Louis Cardinals.

The 1960 Pirates were loaded with champions who came through when they were needed: team captain Dick

Groat at shortstop, Don Hoak at third base, future manager Bill Virdon in centerfield, rock-solid future team captain Bill Mazeroski at second base, and the veteran catcher Smoky Burgess behind the plate. Pitchers Bob Friend, Vernon Law, future pitching coach Harvey Haddix, and the small but commanding relief pitcher of the era, Elroy Face, all led the team in their own right.

Roberto proved again that he was perhaps the best young defensive outfielder in the game, as he threw out 19 base runners during the season.

Tying the Series

In 1960 the Yankees also were having a standout season. Legendary as one of the most overpowering teams ever assembled, the "Bronx Bombers" were led by Mickey Mantle and Roger Maris, who ranked first and second in the American League with 40 and 39 home runs, respectively. The '60 Yankees finished eight games in front of the Baltimore Orioles.

Sports experts gave the Pirates an outside chance to win one game, or possibly two. The Pirates followed through early by taking Game 1 in Forbes Field, 6-4, despite getting outhit, 13-8. Even as Maris and Elston Howard hit home runs for New York, the Pirates' Mazeroski hit a two-run shot in the fourth inning that became the margin of victory.

Mantle roared to life in Game 2 by hitting two home runs and driving in five of the Yankees' 16 runs. Meanwhile, the Pirates scattered 13 hits and scored only three runs. Back in New York for Game 3, the Yankees' Bobby Richardson set a series record by driving in six runs, four on a grand slam. The Pirates future in the series seemed bleak after the 10-0 shutout.

Roberto, as he would through the end of the series and in every World Series game in which he played, hit safely in the three games to that point. In Game 4, Law and relief specialist Face combined to hold New York to eight hits and only two runs. Law also crucially aided his cause, doubling in the first Pirate run, and then scoring the game-deciding run in the three-run fifth inning of the 3-2 victory.

Hustle on Base Paths

In Game 5 the Pirates took a 3-2 series lead with another victory at Yankee Stadium, shocking the nation. Mazeroski, who batted .320 in the series, doubled in two runs in the three-run second inning to give the Pirates the edge in an eventual 5-2 victory.

Back in Pittsburgh Yankee Whitey Ford threw his second shutout in the series, and teammate Bobby Richardson drove in three more runs in a 12-0 Yankee victory in Game 6. In the first six games of the series, the

Yankees had clobbered the Pirates in run totals in victories of 38-3, while the corresponding Pirates' wins totaled 14-8.

Game 7 was a slugfest as Pirates backup first baseman Rocky Nelson hit an early two-run shot and the Yanks' Moose Skowran and Yogi Berra hit home runs. By the bottom of the eighth inning, New York led 7-4. But the Pirates rallied back for five runs and moved ahead, 9-7. The rally might not have lasted, however, if Roberto had not beat out a grounder to first, driving in Gino Cimoli.

Skowran didn't have time to step on first as the speedy Roberto beat him to the bag from the batter's box. Roberto huffed and puffed, catching his breath on first after legging out the most important 90 feet of his life. Groat had moved to third. Backup catcher Hal Smith came to bat. Smith clobbered a three-run homer as the "forgotten hero" of the game, putting Pittsburgh up, 9-7.

Historical Moment

Groat danced over home and Roberto, as one writer described, "came leaping down the line like a kangaroo." Smith was forgotten because the Yankees came back to tie the game 9-9 on three singles and a ground out in the top of the ninth, surviving any way they could.

Mazeroski was the Pirates' first batter in the bottom of the ninth, as 36,683 Forbes Field fans were poised on the edge of their seats and millions more absorbed the drama on television. Yankees pitcher Ralph Terry blew a fastball by Mazeroski and tried to duplicate the feat on the next pitch. Mazeroski swung hard and lofted a ball toward left center field as the TV audience's attention focused on left fielder Yogi Berra. He watched the ball sail above the 406-foot marker and into the parking lot in Schenley Park, which was over the wall from Forbes Field. Yogi turned and trotted for the dugout.

In one of baseball's signature moments, Mazeroski rounded first, pulled off his helmet, and began waving his arms clockwise in elation, attempting to avoid the nearly berserk fans streaming into the base paths. The Pirates were world champions.

After the winning game, Roberto showered and dressed quickly and exited the clubhouse. He celebrated the victory with the fans in the streets of Pittsburgh instead of with his teammates. Roberto had a lot to celebrate: He had led the Pirates that year in runs batted in with 94. He had hit .314 as the league's fourth-best batter. He then averaged .310 in the World Series, hitting in all seven games. He had contributed significantly to the world championship.

Outside Forbes Field in the neighborhood of Oakland, the fans swarmed in ecstasy. "Never had Clemente felt so close to the people of the city," wrote sportswriter Arnold

Hano. "The moment was like a Mardi Gras, a festival, not unlike similar holidays on the streets of San Juan. He walked with the people, mingled, just another human being in the universe of humanity. . . ." Roberto, who had felt like an outsider for so long, later said of the celebration, "I felt like one of them."

Roberto Leads in Hits

Throughout the 1960 World Series, Roberto hit safely in every game. He also posted more hits (nine) than any of his teammates. Roberto took great satisfaction in the season. He had made a major contribution as one of the top hitters and run producers in the National League, and as one of the top players on a team of overachievers. He had achieved the ultimate goal of every team in every season in the nation's most popular sport.

However, after the series, Roberto ended the year in eighth place in the National League's Most Valuable Player voting. Groat was named the MVP. Teammate Don Hoak was second, and Vernon Law also ranked ahead of Clemente—as did Willie Mays, Ernie Banks, Lindy McDaniel, and Ken Boyer. This perceived snub bothered Roberto for years—not because he did not win, but because he ranked so low in the voting.

"I am still bitter," Roberto said years later after winning several batting titles and other personal triumphs.

However, his sense of humor helped take some of the sting away. His teammates started calling him by the nickname "No Votes."

5

LATINO ADVOCATE AND FAMILY MAN

I believe that I can hit with anybody in baseball. Maybe I can't hit with the power of a Mays or a Frank Robinson or a Henry Aaron, but I can hit. As long as I'm in Forbes Field, I can't go for home runs; line drives, yes. I'm a better fielder than anybody you can name. I have great respect for Mays, but I can get a ball like Willie and I have a better arm. I can throw blind to a base.

—Roberto Clemente

The Pirates' tremendous 1960 season was followed by a letdown year in 1961. But Roberto's grit and intelligence led to an extraordinary individual season. He was still the most unpredictable batsman in baseball, but Pirates batting coach George Sisler recognized a method to Roberto's madness. "Clemente's got good common sense," he said. "He uses his intelligence along with his ability."

Roberto led the league in batting for the first time with a .351 average and posted his first 200-hit and 100-run season and his highest slugging percentage (.559). He started his first All-Star Game, drove in the winning run in a 5-4, 11-inning National League victory. For years thereafter he wore his '61 All-Star ring instead of his World Series ring. He came in fourth in the voting for MVP, which was won by Cincinnati's Frank Robinson. Orlando Cepeda and Vada Pinson also were ahead of him.

He logged 27 assists and five double plays. He became notorious for throwing behind base runners. Those 27 remains the most base runners thrown out in a single season since World War II. Dodgers broadcaster Vin Scully once said that Clemente could "field a ball in New York and throw a guy out in Pennsylvania." Roberto was given his first Gold Glove, and many of his fans and fellow players felt that it was about time.

Roberto was voted the Dapper Dan Man of the Year as the sports figure who did the most to promote the city of Pittsburgh, and he was praised for it at the Dapper Dan ceremony, one of the nation's most prestigious annual sporting celebrations.

Puerto Rican Celebration

After the season Roberto and fellow Puerto Rican Orlando Cepeda of the San Francisco Giants, who led the league in home runs (46) and RBIs (142), were treated to a parade through the streets of San Juan by 18,000 fans. The celebration concluded amid a crowd of 5,000 in Sixto Escobar Stadium. Roberto and Orlando were the first Puerto Ricans to lead one of the Major Leagues in a top batting category.

Roberto's baseball prowess grew as players (especially pitchers) and fans in National League cities came to recognize him as a prevalent force in the game. Encouraged by his friend, Pirates radio and television broadcaster Bob Prince, Forbes Field fans began chanting the Spanish slang "Arriba! Arriba!" when he came to bat. In its several contexts, it means "Up there!" "Hurry!" or "Let's go!"

Yet Roberto would remain an enigma with the small-market press in Pittsburgh, which occasionally portrayed him as a hypochondriac who was unwilling to play with injuries. They still quoted him phonetically and amplified his minor differences with Pirates manager Murtaugh, who many times cited the player as the best he had ever seen.

Roberto did not like to play when his 5-foot-11, 180-pound body was not in prime condition. He was a chronic insomniac. He experienced lifelong back pain. When he was sick or nagged by an injury, asking Roberto "How are you?" would mean receiving a very thorough response. "This wasn't a pleasantry to Roberto," remembered Joe L. Brown. "This was a question that you wanted an answer to."

Mr. Aches and Pains

Sportswriter Myron Cope once went to Puerto Rico during the off-season to check on Roberto. At their first meeting Roberto immediately began to explain the chiropractic remedies that he used and extolled throughout his entire career. Cope's story in *Sports Illustrated* about Roberto's aches and pains was accompanied by a graphic that was imitated many times after: a photo of Roberto with many arrows pointing to various body parts labeled with ailments.

At various points Roberto stopped talking to the press. What he did on the field spoke volumes. "If there was a player in memory who let his bat, his glove, his legs, and his arm do the talking, it was Roberto Clemente," said former Pirate and longtime baseball broadcaster Joe Garagiola. "And they were so eloquent."

However, Roberto began to gain a real reputation for arrogance and shirking duty by sitting out games to let his injuries and maladies heal. But if anyone understood his value as a supremely gifted player, it was Roberto himself. And he was not about to present his talent when it was not in good working condition. He refused to walk on the field to give only 80 percent.

"I think the way Clemente played, running out every hit and running recklessly into the wall, he realized he needed some time off and took it," remembered pitcher Bob Friend, whose locker was next to Clemente's for 10 years. "So many times, I saw him catch balls that went into the gap and he'd personally keep the other guy from getting that extra base. For a pitcher, that was something that was really appreciated. An average outfielder will many times give up the extra base. Often that's the difference between winning and losing.

"At Forbes Field, we had one of the toughest right fields to play in baseball. Clemente could play the ball off that cement wall. Clemente could cut off the ball before it could get to the wall; he'd hold it to a single and keep it from being a triple," Friend said.

Showing His Lighter Side

The year 1961 was a critical year for Roberto in terms of his meaning to his team and the game. He was 27 years old. In past years he had already proven himself one of the best hitters and best defensive players in baseball. But in 1960 he was a top all-around Major Leaguer who also helped lead his club to the world championship. Years later Rafael Hernandez Colon, who became governor of

Puerto Rico, recalled the player's development and heroic virtue.

"He had great potential in him as an athlete and as a human being," Colon said. "And he walked through life developing that potential. There was something in Roberto that came out in his movements. This something was the coordination of that soul and that body into an expression of great dignity and great elegance. He always looked like a hero, not only for Puerto Rico. He was the pride of all Latin America. He became someone to emulate."

But Roberto, too, was changing. Others began to detect his lighter, comic side. "I was a real agitator," Friend said. "I'd nail someone's shower shoes to the floor, stuff like that, and Clemente would get a great kick out of it. He enjoyed a good prank."

Roberto won bets that said he could not get undressed from street clothes and into his Pirates uniform inside three minutes. Roberto claimed his six-month 1958 stint in the U.S. Marine Corps Infantry Reserves had given him economy of motion.

"A lot of times he'd run out onto the field with his pants unbuttoned, or his glove on top of his head as he pulled at his belt," remembered Tony Bartirome, a Pirates player in the 1950s who became one of Clemente's closest friends. "And he'd be hollering, 'Where's my glove?

Where's my glove?' I'm telling you, he was a funny, funny man."

Losing Not an Option

One of the funnier and telling stories about Roberto happened in the off-season. Roberto Marin, who had convinced Clemente to play with the Sello Rojo team back in Puerto Rico, asked the star to play on an island softball team against prison inmates. When Marin picked up Clemente at his home, the star was wearing his Pirates uniform. The inmates were impressed. They were less impressed with Marin's pitching and clobbered his pitches.

Roberto, playing shortstop, came to the mound. "Give me the ball," Marin recalled Roberto saying. "I don't even like to lose a game in jail." Marin protested, "But I'm the manager; you can't take me out!" Clemente told him firmly: "Out!"

Roberto struck out several batters as he completed the game. He also drove in the winning runs with a long line drive. "I'm waving the people home, and he comes rounding second base," Marin said. "I signal for him to stop but he slides headfirst into third, and the third baseman goes flying. What a cloud of dust! He gets up, wiping himself off, and I say, 'You're loco! An expensive big leaguer like you, sliding headfirst! And look at that poor prisoner over there; he still hasn't gotten up.'" Roberto responded, "I've always told you I play to win."

Danny Murtaugh wanted Roberto to play through food poisoning, viruses, and the stitched-up wounds the star acquired in collisions with Forbes Field's brick wall or infielders on the base paths. Once Murtaugh wanted him to play with stitches in his ankle. Clemente refused. Murtaugh fined him $150, and that figure jumped in increments of $100 during their heated argument. Murtaugh quit at $650. Roberto paid the fine, and he sat on the bench until the ankle healed.

Helping Latino Players

One thing that Roberto never stopped doing was nurturing and promoting Latin baseball players. With his Latino teammates and Latinos from the other National League clubs, particularly the San Francisco Giants and Milwaukee/Atlanta Braves, which combed Latin America for talent, Roberto became something of a godfather. Players would come to his home for dinner. "Everything is strange" to the Latino new to the United States, Roberto said, particularly in the early 1960s. "The language barrier is great at first. We have trouble ordering food in restaurants. You have no idea how segregation held some of us back. . . . We need time to settle down emotionally. Once we're relaxed and have no problems, we can play baseball

Roberto made the most of his position as a role model for other players and fans. (Corbis)

well. The people who never run into these problems don't have any idea at all what kind of an ordeal it is."

Pitcher Al McBean joined the Pirates in 1961 from the Virgin Islands and became Roberto's roommate. "A lot of Latin players turned to him for advice," McBean said. "He practically set the rules for my conduct. He believes people know you by the company you keep." The Giants great pitcher, Juan Marichal, came to Roberto for back treatments. "He would come into our clubhouse and work on it," Marichal said. "I got three or four adjustments from him. They all helped."

"Roberto was an idol to almost all the Latins, because he fought for the cause of his *campaneros*," said Arturo Garcia, Roberto's chiropractor. "He used to tell me, 'I don't care if they're Puerto Rican or not; they can be Dominican, Venezuelan, Cuban, Mexican—they're Latinos, my people.'" Matty Alou, Jose Pagan, Manny Sanguillen, and others have stories of being treated to bad service in Florida restaurants until the waitstaff recognized that they were with Roberto.

Friendship with Bob Prince

Roberto initiated a lifelong friendship with television broadcaster Bob Prince after several hours of conversation about Prince's call of a heated, late-1950s exchange during a Giants game. Willie Mays had to tackle strapping teammate Orlando Cepeda near the dugout to keep the "Baby Bull" from charging the field. In his broadcast, Prince emphasized several times Cepeda's Puerto Rican nationality in relation to his loss of emotional control. Roberto heard about the broadcast and later convinced Prince that he was playing to the lowest common denominator with clichés about "hotheaded" Latinos. Prince concurred, discovering a side of Clemente that whites rarely saw in those days. In 1971, Roberto presented Prince with the Silver Bat Roberto had received in recognition of the 1961 batting title; Prince cherished the memento for the rest of his life.

Others began to see another side of Roberto. "He was one of the leaders of the Civil Rights movement, of a human movement, in his own way," says sportswriter Arnold Hano. "He was a pioneer for blacks and Latin ballplayers. And we cherish our pioneers."

After a strong 93-68 fourth-place record in 1962, in which Roberto batted .312 for eighth place in the league, both the 1963 and 1964 teams finished dismally. In 1963 the team finished 74-88, 25 games behind the pennant-winning Dodgers, whose Tommy Davis surpassed Roberto in the final month of the season to win the batting title.

Roberto hit .320 on 192 hits and continued his status as a perennial All Star and Gold Glove winner. While the Pirates had another disappointing season in 1964, Roberto won his second batting title with a .339 average and a career- and league-high 211 hits.

Vera Cristina Zabala

Soon Roberto found a better focus for his emotions than the National League umpires, with whom he seemed to have an ongoing feud. (It once led to a $250 fine and suspension delivered by National League president Warren Giles.) During the off-season in 1963 Roberto glimpsed Vera Cristina Zabala in a San Juan drugstore and announced to friends that this beautiful woman would become his wife. Spanish traditions forbade immediate outright courtship, so Roberto conspired with friends of friends to secretly engineer "chance" meetings.

The university-educated Vera, a corporate secretary, was always chaperoned. At first she did not understand baseball, but she learned. A year after Roberto first saw her, Vera married Roberto in the Roman Catholic Church on the plaza in Carolina.

Roberto married Vera Cristina Zabala on November 16, 1964. (Associated Press)

Thousands attended the huge celebration. Roberto bought a multitiered home overlooking San Juan Bay in the Rio Piedras section of San Juan. Here, within a few years, Vera and Roberto would produce, as Kal Wagenheim recalled the kidding of the couple, "a whole outfield of Clementes!" Each one of their three sons, according to Roberto's wishes, was born in Puerto Rico.

6

SUPERSTARDOM

For one thing, I was selected by opponents [for National League Player of the Year]. How would you say it? I was judged by my own peers, and one could hardly expect a greater satisfaction.

—Roberto Clemente

In 1965 the Pittsburgh Pirates received a new manager: Harry "the Hat" Walker. Walker had a distinguished career on the field before becoming a manager, having played for the St. Louis and Philadelphia teams. He was in several World Series and had led the National League in hitting in 1947.

Friends told Roberto that he and the Pirates' talkative new field boss would clash. But Roberto liked to talk hitting, especially with another brother of the bat. Walker advised Clemente in spring training to swing more for the fences.

Bill Mazeroski recalled Walker's words to Roberto: "You're the man, you're the big gun here." This liberated not only

Roberto's swinging power but also his mentoring abilities, which he had exercised selectively under Murtaugh.

Walker treated his number-one player like a partner. But Roberto was not quite ready to play, let alone lead. During the off-season, he was mowing the grass when the blade slammed a rock and ricocheted into his right thigh. Days later, when he ran out a hit in the Winter League All-Star Game, the leg collapsed. A ligament was torn. On January 15 he underwent surgery to drain blood from the leg.

Roberto was absent from spring training. The Pirates announced they were fining their star $100 a day until Vera called to explain that Roberto also was fighting malaria and typhoid fever.

At this point the Great One felt anything but. Ignoring advice to sit out the season, he joined the team in Fort Myers 15 pounds under his 175-pound playing weight. By May his average dipped below .260.

A misunderstanding also flared. Walker told St. Louis broadcaster Harry Caray that "superstars such as Stan Musial and Ted Williams played with injuries." Roberto was infuriated, but agreed to a meeting with Walker in which the partners smoothed things over for the good of the team.

Third Batting Crown

By midseason Clemente was feeling better. He said he would dodge the All-Star Game until Gene Mauch, the

Phillies manager and man in charge of the National League stars, called. "It wouldn't be an All-Star team," Mauch contended, "without Clemente." Sufficiently wooed, Roberto showed up at St. Louis's Busch Stadium and doubled and singled in 105-degree weather for a 2-1 NL victory. He then went on a tear, hitting in 33 of 34 games during the Pirates' resurgence.

Roberto would earn four National League batting titles in his career. (Corbis)

By the end of the 1965 season Roberto eventually hit .329 and won his third batting crown, 11 and 12 points ahead of illustrious runners-up Henry Aaron and Willie Mays. As in 1960 Roberto came in eighth in the MVP voting. He was fourth in the National League with 194 hits, second in triples (14), and sixth in on-base percentage (.378). But the Pirates finished 90-72, behind the Dodgers and Giants.

Clubhouse Leader

Roberto began assuming the role of senior clubhouse spokesman. Broken English or not, he had been in the majors more than a decade. Certainly by example on the field, Clemente was a leader. But at the urging of Walker and general manager Joe L. Brown, Roberto assumed a position of authority.

"Roberto became a leader," Mazeroski said. "He would tell young players what was expected of them. He'd help players who were down. They all looked up to him." As Donn Clendenon remarked: "This was a new Clemente."

Perhaps fatherhood had something to do with that. Roberto spent the winter getting acquainted with his first son. Roberto Jr. had been born on August 17, a day before his dad's own birthday.

The Pirates also received an addition, a "project" for Walker and Clemente. They conspired to make Mateo

"Matty" Rojas Alou, obtained in a trade with the Giants, into a singles-smacking leadoff hitter.

Roberto's status among Latin American players was unparalleled. When he trotted to left field in practice and told the Dominican-born Alou to "hit it to me!" the younger player obliged. Soon, hundreds of low line drives were sailing off Alou's bat over shortstops' leaps.

In a strange example of mentors overtaken by the pupil, Matty Alou, who had hit .231 in 1965, won the 1966 batting title with a .342 average while his big brother, Felipe of the Braves, placed second with a .327 average. His tutor, Roberto, tied Richie Allen for fourth at .317.

Finding the Power Stroke

Roberto tested Walker's idea of his power potential in 1966 by using a lighter bat and pulling the ball more. He proceeded to terrorize opposing pitchers more than ever.

The better they were, the more he liked hitting against them. Sandy Koufax, who felt Clemente was the most unpredictable batter in baseball, offered the best way to pitch to Roberto: "Roll the ball."

Also in 1966 Roberto's powerful bat stroke broke more than premium pitchers' concentrations. On July 15 a lightning drive off his bat back to the mound broke Bob

Gibson's leg. Roberto also hit a three-run homer into the upper deck at Forbes Field off Chicago's Ferguson Jenkins on September 2 for his 2,000th career hit.

The National League pennant-race lead was traded among the Pirates, Dodgers, and Giants until September, when the Pirates settled for 92–70 and, again, third place. But the year's ride seemed to lighten Roberto's mood.

Vernon Law recalled the more jovial Roberto: "Besides being a great ballplayer, he had an infectious smile and was pleasant to be around. He enjoyed a good laugh and at times could be a real prankster, not only in the clubhouse, but at the hotels where we stayed."

MVP at Last

The Pirates led the majors in 1966 with a batting average of .279. And Clemente led the Pirates in spirit and nearly everything else. In his quest for power, his average dipped a bit to .317, but he had career highs with 29 home runs and 119 RBIs.

He was second in the league in RBIs, total bases (342), and extra-base hits (71); third in hits (202) and triples (11); fourth in runs (105), times on base (248), and batting; fifth in home runs and doubles (31); sixth in at-bats (638); and seventh in strikeouts (109). He again led both leagues in assists by outfielders (17).

Roberto's extraordinary year was, this time, given its full measure by the Baseball Writers' Association of America. The legendary Koufax had his greatest season, leading the league with 27 wins, 317 strikeouts, 1.73 earned run average, 27 complete games, and five shutouts. But Roberto Clemente was named the National League's Most Valuable Player.

"I think he was the MVP because he did so many little things, things that some stars don't do," Harry Walker said, citing Roberto's "hustling on routine ground balls, breaking up double plays, and hustling to take an extra base. He set an example that others followed."

Ethnic and Racial Issues

Roberto never lost sight of his status as an example that others followed. He always had an awareness of his position as the most significant Latino athlete and certainly one of the most prominent black athletes in America.

His exploits were routinely discussed the next day in Mexico, across the Caribbean, and in the United States. Whether Pittsburgh won or lost was insignificant compared to "el Magnifico" going 2 for 4. "What did Clemente do?" was a daily question in Pittsburgh and San Juan.

After the November 16 MVP announcement reporters found Roberto atop a bulldozer on his farm. He said he expected to win and then focused on his dream to build a "sports city" for underprivileged children. His second son, Luis Roberto, had been born on July 13, 1966.

"This makes me happy, because now the people feel that if I could do it, then they could do it," Roberto said. "The kids have someone to look to and to follow. That's why I like to work with kids so much. I show them what baseball has done for me, and maybe they will work harder and try harder to be better men."

Roberto's MVP win was another sign of the changing times in the United States and in baseball: The number of Latinos in the majors more than doubled during the late 1960s.

"Clemente was really the first of the Puerto Rican superstars who broke through into mainstream American consciousness for the Puerto Rican people," media personality Geraldo Rivera recalled. "It was a source of tremendous pride to have someone with tremendous success and skill. It made all of us proud."

Clemente used the attention to sound off on race relations. Two years after the Civil Rights Act of 1964 Roberto talked about racial equality with a statesman's tone rather than passion.

"The Latin American player doesn't get the recognition he deserves," Roberto said. "Neither does the Negro player, unless he does something really spectacular, like

Willie Mays. We have self-satisfaction, yes. But after the season, nobody cares about us.

"Juan Marichal is one of the greatest pitchers in the game, but does he get invited to banquets?" Roberto asked. "Somebody says we live too far away. That's a lousy excuse. I am an American citizen. But some people act like they think I live in the jungle someplace. To the people, we are outsiders, foreigners."

Among the Elite's Elite

Roberto's salary, however, was very competitive with other players in the National League. He became the first Pirate and one of the first Major Leaguers to earn more than $100,000 a year, joining the ranks of Mays, Aaron, Mantle, and Frank Robinson. In 1967 Roberto opened a restaurant in Puerto Rico. He also started to open up personally to his teammates. "You could see him change," catcher Jim Pagliaroni said.

Roberto raised his average by 40 points in 1967 while retaining the power stroke, as the Pirates continued to outhit everyone with a .277 team average.

On May 15 Roberto hit three homers and a double to drive in all seven Pirate runs against the Reds, who scored eight and won the game. After giving the greatest one-game performance of his career, Roberto said, "I would rather win."

The Pirates' long season ended at 81-81, putting them in sixth place. Roberto led the majors with 209 hits and a career-high .357 average to win his fourth batting title. His power numbers were down from 1966, but he still had 23 home runs and 110 RBIs—one off the league-leading 111 by Orlando Cepeda of St. Louis, who won the pennant.

Roberto batting against the New York Mets (Corbis)

Cepeda won the MVP, which meant Puerto Ricans won the award in back-to-back years. Roberto placed third behind St. Louis catcher Tim McCarver.

Shoulder Injury

The Pirates, under new manager Larry Shepard, stayed nearly the same in 1968, in sixth place at 80-82. The biggest change was not for the better. One day Roberto was climbing a wall from his lower patio to the upper one when the iron bar he grabbed to help hoist him up gave way. He tumbled down a steep embankment.

"I must have rolled 75 to 100 feet until another wall stopped me," he said. "I went over on my shoulder several times." He rejected his doctor's advice to wear a shoulder brace.

Vera told him not to quit when he was down. "If you want to quit after another year, I won't say a word," she told him. The season was atypical for Roberto. By May he was benched. He then told skeptical reporters about his accident. He batted .245 at midyear and did not make the All-Star Game. He worried about his future. "People say I'm moody," he told *Life* magazine. "But if I don't take care of myself, I'm stealing people's money. My conscience wouldn't stand that."

He returned to the lineup and his average eventually reached .291—10th in the league, a terrific year for a good player. But Clemente had not hit that low since 1958.

Almost a Fifth Title

One of the game's great triples hitters, Roberto led the Majors for the only time in that category with 12 in 1969 as his shoulder healed. And he provided the only drama for the again third-place Pirates by contending for his possible fifth batting title.

The competition was Cleon Jones of the pennant-winning Mets and Cincinnati's Pete Rose, known as "Charlie Hustle," who had ended four straight years of Pirates' batting-title wins when he copped the 1968 crown with a .335 average.

With a week to go in the season, Jones batted .346, Rose .344, and Roberto .335. Roberto got three hits in a doubleheader against the Phillies, six hits in a three-game stand against the Cubs, and five in the final two games against the Montreal Expos.

Roberto hit .538 during the final week to elevate his average an amazing 10 points to .345. But Rose's last at-bat of the season was true to Charlie Hustle tradition: He beat out a bunt to post a .348 average and win the title. Rose gave credit where it was due. Of his dueling mate for the '69 batting title, he said, "I'd say he's the best hitter I've ever seen since I've been in the big leagues."

7

"THE GAME IS TRULY HIS"

I want everybody in the world to know that this is the way I play all the time. All season, every season. I gave everything I had to this game.

—Roberto Clemente

The Pittsburgh Pirates were changing on all fronts. Their new spring-training facility had opened at Bradenton, Florida, in 1969. Three Rivers Stadium, their $45 million new home field, replaced the legendary Forbes Field. The new stadium dominated the city's north side just across the Allegheny River from downtown. On the stadium's inaugural day, July 16, 1970, the Pirates donned new stretch uniforms. Also, Danny Murtaugh had returned for his second stint as manager of the team.

Meanwhile, Roberto had expanded his experience in the game by managing the San Juan Senators in the

Puerto Rican Winter League. There he came to understand the psychology and peculiarities of the kind of job that he could have had in his Major League future.

The Pirates also welcomed some new faces, including line-drive-smashing lefty Al Oliver, dexterous catcher Manny Sanguillen, and infielders Richie Hebner, Dave Cash, and slugger Bob Robertson. Willie Stargell kept improving to solidify his reputation as a premier power hitter.

Roberto, at age 34, was the grand old man of the club—a year older than Bill Mazeroski. And this "old man" never stopped exercising his role as a mentor for younger players.

"He wanted me to take a look at what was going on for the guys who were coming up, and to try and show them the way he showed me," pitcher Dock Ellis recalled. "He brought the winning attitude: 'We are going to win every day.' And that's what he did."

Roberto Clemente Night

The 1970 Pirates clinched the National League's Eastern Division Championship, but they lost in the divisional playoffs to another developing dynasty, the Cincinnati Reds.

At several points during the year the top 10 batters in the league consisted of five Reds and five Pirates, which included Roberto. He hit .352 that year, but he was hampered by nagging injuries and missed 54 games.

A highlight of the 1970 season for both the club and Roberto was staged on July 24, which was declared "Roberto Clemente Night." During the Pirates' 11-0 victory over the Houston Astros, Roberto singled twice and added one of his patented sliding catches near the bull pen off the bat of Denis Menke. And all of that came after the Pirates gave "the Great One" a fitting hour-long tribute.

"They gave him so many things, and said so many nice things—when all of those thousands of people stood

Roberto and his family at Roberto Clemente Night
(Associated Press)

up and cheered, well, Roberto let loose with a torrent of tears," remembered Juan Jimenez, a Puerto Rican representative at the event. Jimenez had collected 300,000 signatures in an enormous urn from about a third of Puerto Rico's population to celebrate the island's favorite son. "And when he spoke," Jimenez continued, "everyone else cried. . . .When he finished, I thought the stadium would collapse from the cheers and applause."

Ten Hits in Two Games

On August 23, 1970, Roberto entered the record books again by performing a feat that had not happened yet in the 20th century: He clubbed 10 hits in two consecutive games. On August 22 Roberto went 5 for 7 against the Dodgers. He drove in one run and scored the other in the 2-1 win. The next day in Los Angeles, he went 5 for 6 to lead an 11-0 Pirates victory. Roberto homered, doubled, scored four runs, and drove in three.

In 1971 things kept getting better for the Pirates. The team's pitching finally blossomed as Ellis won 19 games and Steve Blass won 15. Dave Giusti led the National League with 30 saves. This time the team was not going to let insufficient pitching sink the ship, as they acquired Nelson Briles from St. Louis and Bob Johnson from Kansas City. Stargell led the league with 48 home runs and drove in 125 runs, while Roberto hit .341 with 86 RBIs. Stargell and Clemente both finished as top-five MVP vote-getters (St. Louis's Joe Torre was selected for that top honor).

The 1971 season also marked an important turning point for Roberto and all minority baseball players. Historian Bruce Markusen remarked that the events of September 1, 1971, remain "one of the most significant milestones in the racial history of Major League Baseball." That night Pittsburgh fielded the first all-minority lineup in Major League history. "I'm color blind," Murtaugh said, shrugging. The media at Three Rivers noticed that Clemente, Stargell, and Gene Clines played the outfield; Oliver, Cash, Jackie Hernandez, and Rennie Stennett were in the infield; Sanguillen caught, and Ellis pitched. Roberto went 2 for 4 and he, Stargell, and Sanguillen, who homered, each had two RBIs. The Pirates beat Philadelphia in that game, 10-7.

New Players to Mentor

The new group of Pirates came to rely on Roberto both on the field and off. His impact on some was lasting. Al "Scoop" Oliver, who would go on collect an impressive 2,743 hits in 18 years in the big leagues, said, "Outside of my parents, Roberto had the biggest impact on me. He might have been the only one in the organization who understood me. He was raised the same way. He proved you could have an ego and not be egotistical—confident but not cocky, humble when [he] needed to be, but, most of all, maintaining your dignity and self-respect in spite of all the negative obstacles that were in his way."

Indeed, no obstacle ever stopped Roberto from excelling at baseball. It was his job, his livelihood, his vocation, and his great source of pride. "Clemente," Roger Angell once wrote in *The New Yorker*, "has no sense of humor about baseball." In a game that takes 162 games per year across most of the calendar plus spring training, Roberto Clemente always performed at a peak level.

Instilling Confidence

The Pirates, who were the Eastern Division champions in 1971, defeated the San Francisco Giants 9-5 in the final game of the five-game league playoff series. The Baltimore Orioles had captured the American League pennant on the arms of the first group of four 20-game winners in nearly two decades: Dave McNally (21-5), Pat Dobson (20-8), Jim Palmer (20-9), and Mike Cuellar (20-9). The Orioles were heavily favored to win. Baseball fans wondered whether or not the Pirates could get enough hits to win even a game against the Orioles.

The one questionable link in the regular Pirate lineup was Jackie Hernandez, who had inherited shortstop from injured Gene Alley. But the Cuban-born Hernandez was a career .208 hitter who had been a big-league starter once, in 1969. Down the homestretch, Hernandez seemed to have even lost his defensive edge, booting several key ground balls. People wondered how he was even going to start in the World Series.

Roberto had mentored dozens of players like Hernandez who needed help. But instilling confidence in Hernandez was no easy task, as the player was very nervous about his performance. "I felt like spending the whole night in the clubhouse," Hernandez said, remembering one evening spent in tears at his locker. "I didn't want to go outside." Roberto consoled him, became his friend, and revitalized the shortstop's confidence. Hernandez later credited Roberto's counseling with his sharp series play.

Holding On for Victory

In the first game of the 1971 World Series Baltimore breezed to victory, 5-3. Roberto doubled and singled for two-thirds of the Pirates' hits, while the Orioles clubbed three home runs. A sweep seemed possible after Baltimore also took Game 2, 11-3. Roberto was the only Pirate with multiple hits, duplicating his Game 1 tally of a double and single.

Back at Three Rivers Stadium for Game 3, pitcher Steve Blass hurled a three-hitter and Pittsburgh prevailed, 5-1. Roberto drove in one run and Robertson clouted a three-run home run. The series was evened on October 13 in a tightly contested 4-3 Pirates victory. Bruce Kison tossed a four-hitter as the Pirates sprayed 14 hits and Clemente went 3 for 4.

Playing on their home turf revitalized the Pirates. To cap it, Nelson Briles threw a 4-0 two-hitter, hurling so hard at times that he occasionally flung himself to the ground. Jackie Hernandez, having overcome his obstacles with a 2 for 3 day, was the only Pirate with more than one hit. For Game 6, the teams moved back to Baltimore, where the Orioles evened the series with a 3-2 victory in 10 innings. Roberto homered and tripled in the loss and pre-

Roberto hits a home run during Game Six of the 1971 World Series. (Associated Press)

vented a ninth-inning run from scoring when he unleashed a shot to hold a runner on third.

In the seventh and deciding game Blass again held on for a 2-1 victory, surviving some dramatics in the eighth inning to win on eight pitches in the ninth. The final out, a grounder deep to short, was snapped over to first by the revitalized Hernandez. Pandemonium reigned. Blass leaped off the mound and kept leaping—into Robertson's arms. Sanguillen flapped his arms like a berserk bird around the infield, still clutching mitt and mask. Clemente bolted for the dugout as the fans swarmed onto the field past security guards.

The Pirates were again world champions. Despite the underrated Pittsburgh pitching against the supposedly overpowering Orioles, the series is usually described in terms of Clemente. "He was electrical, and it was magnetic," Briles said.

In the series Clemente led all hitters with a .414 average, 12 hits, five extra-base hits, two home runs, and four runs scored. He was named the series' Most Valuable Player. His was one of the most outstanding performances in World Series history. "Now," he told the press, "everyone knows the way Roberto Clemente plays. I believe I am the best player in baseball today. and I am glad that I was able to show it against Baltimore in the World Series."

"Now and again, very rarely, we see a man who seems to have met all the demands, challenged all the implacable averages, spurned the mere luck," wrote Roger Angell. "He has defied baseball, even altered it. And for a time, at least, the game is truly his."

8

ADIOS, ROBERTO

I would be lost without baseball. I don't think I could stand being away from it as long as I was alive.

—Roberto Clemente

The 1972 Pirates were considered even better than the 1971 world championship team. Clemente was injured part of the year and only played in 102 games, hitting .312 with 60 RBIs. He still made the All-Star team and won his 12th consecutive Gold Glove Award by posting his first errorless season: 1.000 percent on 199 putouts.

But for the first time since the 1960 World Championship, he was not absolutely required to shoulder a large share of the responsibility or heroics. Roberto did, however, enjoy honorary days during the 1972 campaign. He passed Honus Wagner as the Pirates' all-time hit leader and then collected his 3,000th hit on September 30.

A stand-up double marked that milestone against the Mets at Three Rivers Stadium. Roberto stood, one foot on the bag, as he raised his hat to a standing ovation that lasted several minutes. The Great One put his hands on his hips and rolled his head around to relieve the pressure on his neck. Umpire Doug Harvey handed Roberto the ball and shook the hand of only the 11th man in history to reach 3,000.

The double sparked a three-run rally and the Pirates eventually won. Roberto played one inning more as the fans cheered him in the outfield. Roberto's old pal Willie Mays came over to congratulate his old outfield mate.

True Happiness

As usual, Roberto exhibited pride and dignity. But the veterans realized the enormity of the event for Roberto. Jose Pagan tried to relieve tension beforehand by volunteering to get the hit himself for Roberto. Willie Stargell actually handed Roberto the bat that day, saying, "Here, use this." Manny Sanguillen watched the proud and reserved Roberto through all of the impromptu ceremonies. "But after the ballgame is over," the catcher said years later, "you can see [in Clemente] the rejoicing, the true happiness."

Baseball was Roberto's stage to the world. In the rare moments of honor to be cherished, he was impeccable.

Hitting number 3,000 meant more to Roberto than a great indicator of his precise batting skills and longevity. He had not spent nearly half of his life in Pittsburgh just to pile up impressive numbers.

"To get 3,000 hits means you've got to play a lot," Roberto said. "To me, it means more. I know how I am and what I've been through. I don't want to get 3,000 hits to pound my chest and holler, 'Hey, I got it.' What it means is that I didn't fail with the ability I had. I've seen lots of players come and leave. Some failed because they don't

Roberto makes his 3,000th hit. (National Baseball Library, Cooperstown, N.Y.)

have the ability. And some failed because they don't have the desire."

Playing for his old outfield mate, Bill Virdon, who replaced Danny Murtaugh as the Pirates' manager, Roberto contributed to the team when he could. By September 22 the Pirates had won the National League East with a Major League–leading .274 team batting average.

Shocking End to Big Season

But the world champions and their confident fans were in for a shock. In the League Championship Series against the Cincinnati Reds, the teams traded wins through four contests. Sanguillen homered in Game 3 and then drove in the winning run in the eighth inning. In Game 4 the Pirates were stonewalled by Ross Grimsley, who went the distance with a two-hitter, 7-1.

Game 5 was the Pirates' to take. They led the contest through eight innings. But in the ninth inning the Reds outstanding catcher, Johnny Bench, homered to tie the game at 3-3.

And then Tony Perez and Denis Menke singled. Bob Moose was brought in as the reliever. He retired two batters, but George Foster, running for Perez, reached third on a fly out. The game and pennant sailed away from the Pirates on the next throw, a wild pitch. Foster scored, and the Reds went to the World Series.

The disappointing 1972 playoff finale left a bittersweet impression on Blass, the Pirates' ace with a 19-8 season. "[Clemente] came around to everybody's locker," Blass remembered. "He said, 'Keep your head up, keep your head up. We are a very good baseball team. We had a very good year.'

"Well, we all knew that and could feel that," Blass said. "But here's a guy who has the . . . inspiration, to say it, to take the time to go around to everybody's locker and say that. It's not going to change that, but, here, 21 years later, you remember that."

The Harsh News

Sadly, that was one of the last times Roberto's teammates saw him. Less than three months later he was gone. Sketchy reports of the plane crash reached New Year's Eve parties in Pennsylvania. U.S. Navy divers eventually found the wreckage of the overloaded DC-7 120 feet below the surface and recovered only one of Roberto's socks and his briefcase.

The Baseball Hall of Fame amended its procedures and waived the five-year waiting rule specifically for Roberto on January 3. Newspaper editorials as well as Baseball Commissioner Bowie Kuhn and fans throughout America supported the waiver.

Roberto's wife, sons, and mother at his induction into the Baseball Hall of Fame (National Baseball Hall of Fame Library, Cooperstown, N.Y.)

A story told by Pittsburgh sportswriter Al Abrams was eerily recycled. Clemente visited the Hall of Fame on July 22, 1968, and snapped photos of exhibits. A fan saw him and remarked, "This is where you belong." Roberto thanked the fan, then said, "I guess a fellow like me has to die to get voted in by the writers."

The Pirates chartered a plane to San Juan. On January 4, 1973, Blass delivered the eulogy in San Fernando Catholic Church in Roberto's hometown of Carolina.

Working for the Greater Good

Pirates pitcher Steve Blass said, "Clemente performed so well that even if you felt as if you weren't as talented or as gifted as him, that it was kind of embarrassing not to try. I think he lifted you a little bit by just trying to keep up with him in terms of effort."

Extra effort was a Roberto Clemente hallmark, and not just when it came to stretching a double into a triple or taking away a hit by crashing into a wall. Roberto's special projects—such as building a sports city for kids in San Juan and taking over the Managua earthquake efforts—were full-effort undertakings that required all his energies. Sports City was eventually realized in 1974 as his family and San Juan officials followed through on his wishes to create the athletic complex for youngsters. "He was a giver," Willie Stargell said. "He wanted to help wherever there was help needed."

To be equipped with a great athlete's strength and quickness is one thing. To put in the effort to maximize those gifts is something more. To use those things to achieve other greater goods—team accomplishments as well as promoting regional, racial, and ethnic pride and help for the less gifted—is quite another.

Roberto was able to achieve the greater things because of his confidence in his abilities, his sense of pride, thorough belief in competition, and dedication to an unceasing work ethic.

"I love competition," Roberto told an audience late in his life, "because when a person is faced with competition, he has to struggle that much harder to be a winner. A winner is proud, and that's the sound foundation on which our nation was built. . . . No one hands it to you on a silver platter. It's a struggle for survival, and no one, with a goal in mind, can afford to let up. Everyone knows I have been struggling all my life. I believe that every human being is equal, but one has to fight hard all the time to maintain that equality."

He died fighting for that equality.

"Roberto Clemente is our Jackie Robinson," said All-Star shortstop Alex Rodriguez, one of many stars who looked to Roberto Clemente's life as a source of spiritual

Roberto will always be remembered for working for the greater good, both on and off the field. (Associated Press)

stimulus. "He was a big inspiration for what he did on and off the field—for everyone. The way he died on the battlefield, helping out thousands of people, was really indicative of what his whole life was all about."

TIME LINE

1934   Born in Carolina, Puerto Rico, on August 18, the youngest of seven children, to Melchor Clemente and Luisa Walker

1948   Begins playing organized ball at age 14 as shortstop for Sello Rojo, a rice company softball team

1951   Baseball and track star at Julio C. Vizarrondo High School

1952   Signs first professional contract with semipro Santurce Cangrejeros (Crabbers), Puerto Rican Winter League, for $40 a week

1954   Signs $5,000 contract (with a $10,000 bonus) with Brooklyn Dodgers, farmed out to minor league Montreal Royals; becomes first draft choice on November 22 of last-place Pittsburgh Pirates, who claim him for $4,000

1955   In first Major League at-bat on April 17, singles in the Pittsburgh home-opener against the Dodgers and scores a run; hits .255 for the rookie season as the Pirates' starting right fielder

1956   Bats .300 or better (.311) for the first of 13 times, placing third in the league behind Henry Aaron and outfield mate Bill Virdon; off-season auto accident in Puerto Rico leaves him with lifelong back ailments

1957   Hits .396 in 225 at-bats for the Santurce Cangrejeros club during the off-season in the Puerto Rican Winter League for the highest pro average of his career; bats .253 on the year for the Pirates

1958   Leads National League outfielders in assists (22) for the first time; sets NL record with three triples in a game on September 8 against Cincinnati; bats .289; sworn in for six months of Marine Corps Reserve training on September 13

1959   On disabled list from May 25 through July 3 after being hit on the elbow with a pitch; bats .296 on the year

1960   Plays major role in the Pirates' World Series victory over the New York Yankees; leads team with

94 RBIs and Majors with 19 outfield assists; bats .314 on the season for National League fourth place and .310 in the World Series, hitting in all seven games; was roster selection for both All-Star Games; named National League Player of the Month for May

1961   Wins first batting title with a .351 average and posts highest outfielder assist total since World War II with 27, and no one has thrown out as many runners since; also posts his first 200-hit and 100-run season and a career-high .559 slugging percentage while winning the first of 12 consecutive Gold Gloves; in his first of 12 All-Star Games as a starter, singles in the winning run in a 5-4 National League victory and plays all 11 innings

1962   Receives first Dapper Dan Award as Pittsburgh's Sportsman of the Year for 1961 on February 4; hits .312

1963   His .320 average places him second in National League batting; has three hits in All-Star Game won by the NL, 5-3

1964   Meets Vera Zabala in San Juan, they become engaged prior to spring training and marry on November 14 in Carolina, Puerto Rico; wins second batting title with a .339 average and leads league with 211 hits

1965   First son, Roberto Walker Clemente Jr., is born August 17; wins third batting title with a .329 average

1966   Second son, Luis Roberto, born July 13; wins National League Most Valuable Player Award with a .317 average, 202 hits, 29 home runs, 119 RBIs and 342 total bases as well as a Majors-leading 17 assists; presented David L. Lawrence Award for promoting the city of Pittsburgh; drives Ferguson Jenkins fastball into Forbes Field's upper deck for 2,000th career hit on September 2

1967   Receives second Dapper Dan Award on January 29; wins fourth batting title with his highest ever Major League average of .357, again leads league in hits (209) and assists (17, for a National League record-breaking and Major League–tying fifth time) and is one RBI shy of fellow Puerto Rican Orlando Cepeda's league-leading 111; named NL Player of the Month for May

1968   Off-season muscle tear in right shoulder hampers productivity; bats .291

1969   Third son, Roberto Enrique, born May 20; misses fifth
batting title by three percentage points with .345
average and leads league in triples (12); named
National League Player of the Month for July

1970   Celebrated on Roberto Clemente Night, July 24, at
Three Rivers Stadium; becomes first player since
1900 to collect 10 hits in two consecutive games (5
for 7, 5 for 6 vs. Dodgers) on August 23; hits .352 on
the year

1971   Leads Pirates to the world championship over the
Baltimore Orioles with a showcase performance in
the World Series, hitting .414 and in all seven
games, once again to tie Major League record;
named series MVP; bats .341 on the year with 86
RBIs

1972   Becomes the 11th player in baseball history to collect 3,000 hits with a double in final regular-season
game September 30; becomes Pirates all-time hits
leader September 2 with number 2,971, breaking
Honus Wagner's team record; bats .312; dies
December 31 in plane crash off Puerto Rico

1973   Inducted into the Baseball Hall of Fame at
Cooperstown, New York, August 6, the first

Latin American to earn the honor by a special ballot that waived the five-year retirement rule; Baseball Commissioner Bowie Kuhn creates the Roberto Clemente Award for sportsmanship and community activism; Pirates officially retire number 21 on Opening Day, April 6, at Three Rivers Stadium; receives the inaugural Presidential Citizens Medal, accepted by Vera Clemente, from President Richard M. Nixon in an Oval Office ceremony May 14; becomes first ballplayer to be posthumously honored by U.S. Mint

1974 Roberto Clemente *Ciudad Deportivo* (Sports City) created in San Juan

1994 Pirates unveil Roberto Clemente statue at Three Rivers Stadium

1999 Named number 71 of ESPN's Top 100 Athletes of the 20th Century

2002 Inducted into the Hall of Black Achievement in Bridgewater, Massachusetts, on January 31; Baseball Commissioner Bud Selig proclaims September 18 "Roberto Clemente Day" during Hispanic Heritage Month; in November the Hall of Fame plaque is recast to rightfully depict proper birth name, Roberto Clemente Walker

2003   Awarded the Presidential Medal of Freedom, the highest civilian honor in the United States, by President George W. Bush

2004   Voted "Top Player" in the history of the Pirates by a vote of the fans conducted by Major League Baseball, receiving 63 percent of the votes, and 78 percent of the votes as the top outfielder

HOW TO BECOME A PROFESSIONAL ATHLETE

THE JOB

Unlike amateur athletes who play or compete in amateur circles for titles or trophies only, professional athletic teams compete against one another to win titles, championships, and series; team members are paid salaries and bonuses for their work.

The athletic performances of individual teams are evaluated according to the nature and rules of each specific sport: Usually the winning team compiles the highest score, as in football, basketball, and soccer. Competitions are organized by local, regional, national, and international organizations and associations whose primary functions are to promote the sport and sponsor competitive events. Within a professional sport there are usually different levels of competition based on age, ability, and gender. There are often different designations and divisions within one sport. Professional baseball, for example, is made up of the two major leagues (American and National) each made up of three divisions, East, Central, and West; and the minor leagues (single-A, double-A, triple-A). All of these teams are considered professional because the players are compensated for their work, but the financial rewards are the greatest in the Major Leagues.

Whatever the team sport, most team members specialize in a specific area of the game. In gymnastics, for example, the entire six-member team trains on all of the gymnastic apparatuses—balance beam, uneven bars, vault, and floor exercise—but usually each of the six gymnasts excels in only one or two areas. Those gymnasts who do excel in all four events are likely to do well in the individual all-around title, which is a part of the team competition. Team members in football, basketball, baseball, soccer, and hockey all assume different positions, some of which change depending on whether or not the team is trying to score a goal (offensive positions) or prevent the opposition from scoring one (defensive positions). During team practices, athletes focus on their specific role in a game, whether that is defensive, offensive, or both. For example, a pitcher will spend some time running bases and throwing to other positions, but the majority of his or her time will most likely be spent practicing pitching.

Professional teams train for most of the year, but unlike athletes in individual sports, the athletes who are members of a team usually have more of an off-season. The training programs of professional athletes differ according to the season. Following an off-season, most team sports have a training season, in which they begin to focus their workouts after a period of relative inactivity to develop or maintain strength, cardiovascular ability, flexibility, endurance, speed, and quickness, as well as to focus on technique and control. During the season, the team coach, physician, trainers, and physical therapists organize specific routines, programs, or exercises to target game skills as well as individual athletic weaknesses, whether skill-related or from injury.

These workouts also vary according to the difficulty of the game schedule. During a playoff or championship series, the coach and athletic staff realize that a rigorous workout in between games might tax the athletes' strength, stamina, or even mental preparedness, jeopardizing the outcome of the next game. Instead, the coach might prescribe a mild workout followed by intensive stretching. In addition to stretching and exercising the specific muscles used in any given sport, athletes concentrate on developing excellent eating and sleeping habits that will help them remain in top condition throughout the year. Abstaining from drinking alcoholic beverages during a season is a practice to which many professional athletes adhere.

The coaching or training staff often films the games and practices so that the team can benefit from watching their individual exploits, as well as their combined play. By watching their performances, team members can learn how to improve their techniques and strategies. It is common for professional teams to also study other teams' moves and strategies in order to determine a method of coping with the other teams' plays during a game.

REQUIREMENTS
High School
Most professional athletes demonstrate tremendous skill and interest in their sport well before high school. High school offers student athletes the opportunity to gain experience in the field in a structured and competitive environment. Under the guidance of a coach, you can begin developing suitable training programs for yourself and learn about health, nutrition, and conditioning issues.

High school also offers you the opportunity to experiment with a variety of sports and a variety of positions within a sport. Most junior varsity and some varsity high school teams allow you to try out different positions and begin to discover whether you have more of an aptitude for the defensive dives of a goalie or for the forwards' front-line action. High school coaches will help you learn to expand upon your strengths and abilities and develop yourself more fully as an athlete. High school is also an excellent time to begin developing the concentration powers, leadership skills, and good sportsmanship necessary for success in the field.

People who hope to become professional athletes should take a full load of high school courses including four years of English, math, and science as well as health and physical education. A solid high school education will help ensure success in college (often the next step in becoming a professional athlete) and may help you in earning a college athletic scholarship. A high school diploma will certainly give you something to fall back on if an injury, a change in career goals, or other circumstance prevents you from earning a living as an athlete.

Postsecondary Training

College is important for future professional athletes for several reasons. It provides the opportunity to gain skill and strength in your sport before you try to succeed in the pros, and it also offers you the chance of being observed by professional scouts.

Perhaps most importantly, however, a college education arms you with a valuable degree that you can use if you do not earn a living as a professional athlete or after your performance career ends. College athletes major in everything from communications to premed and enjoy careers as coaches, broadcasters, teachers, doctors, actors, and businesspeople, to name a few. As with high school sports, college athletes must maintain certain academic standards in order to be permitted to compete in intercollegiate play.

Other Requirements

If you want to be a professional athlete, you must be fully committed to succeeding. You must work almost nonstop to improve your conditioning and skills and not give up when you do not succeed as quickly or as easily as you had hoped. And even then, because the competition is so fierce, the goal of earning a living as a professional athlete is still difficult to reach. For this reason, professional athletes must not get discouraged easily. They must have the self-confidence and ambition to keep working and keep trying. Professional athletes must also have a love for their sport that compels them to want to reach their fullest potential.

EXPLORING

Students interested in pursuing a career in professional sports should start playing that sport as much and as early as possible. Most junior high and high schools have well-established programs in the sports that have professional teams.

If a team sport does not exist in your school that does not mean your chances at playing it have evaporated. Petition your school board to establish it as a school sport and set aside funds for it. In the meantime organize other students into a club team, scheduling practices and unofficial games. If the sport is a recognized team sport in the United States or Canada, contact the professional organization for the sport for additional information; if anyone would have helpful tips for gaining recognition, the professional organization would. Also, try calling the local or state athletic board to see what other schools in your area recognize it as a team sport; make a list of those teams and try scheduling exhibition games with them. Your goal is to show that other students have a definite interest in the game and that other schools recognize it.

To determine if you really want to commit to pursuing a professional career in your team sport, talk to coaches, trainers, and any athletes who are currently pursuing a professional career. You can also contact professional organizations and associations for information on how to best prepare for a career in their sport. Sometimes there are specialized training programs available, and the best way to find out is to get in contact with the people whose job it is to promote the sport.

EMPLOYERS

Professional athletes are employed by private and public ownership groups throughout the United States and Canada. At the highest male professional level, there are 32 National Football League franchises, 30 Major League Baseball franchises, 29 National Basketball Association franchises, 30 National Hockey League franchises, and 10 Major League Soccer franchises. The Women's National Basketball Association has 13 franchises.

STARTING OUT

Most team sports have some official manner of establishing which teams acquire which players; often, this is referred to as a draft, although sometimes members of a professional team are chosen through a competition. Usually, the draft occurs between the college and professional levels of the sport. The National Basketball Association (NBA), for example, has its NBA College Draft. During the draft, the owners and managers of professional basketball teams choose players in an order based on the team's performance in the previous season. This means that the team with the worst record in the previous season has a greater chance of getting to choose first from the list of available players.

Furthermore, professional athletes must meet the requirements established by the organizing bodies of their respective sport. Sometimes this means meeting a physical requirement, such as age, height, and weight; sometimes this means fulfilling a number of required stunts, or participating in a certain number of competitions. Professional organizations usually arrange it so that athletes can build up their skills and level of play by participating in lower-level competitions. College sports, as mentioned before, are an excellent way to improve one's skills while pursuing an education.

ADVANCEMENT

Professional athletes in team sports advance in three ways: when their team advances, when they are traded to better teams, and when they negotiate better contracts. In all three instances this is achieved by the individual team member who works and practices hard, and who gives his or her best performance in game after game. Winning teams also receive a deluge of media attention that often creates celebrities out of individual players, which in turn provides these top players with opportunities for financially rewarding commercial endorsements.

Professional athletes are usually represented by sports agents in the behind-the-scenes deals that determine for which teams they will be playing and what they will be paid. These agents may also be involved with other key decisions involving commercial endorsements, personal income taxes, and financial investments of the athlete's revenues.

In the moves from high school athletics to collegiate athletics and from collegiate athletics to the pros, coaches and scouts are continually scouring the ranks of high school and college teams for new talent; they are most interested in the athletes who consistently deliver points or prevent the opposition from scoring. There is simply no substitute for success.

A college education, however, can prepare all athletes for the day when their bodies can no longer compete at the top level, whether because of age or an unforeseen injury. Every athlete should be prepared to move into another career, related to the world of sports or not.

Professional athletes do have other options, especially those who have graduated from a four-year college or university. Many go into some area of coaching, sports administration, management, or broadcasting. The professional athlete's unique insight and perspective can be a real asset in these careers. Other athletes simultaneously pursue other interests, some completely unrelated to their sport, such as education, business, social welfare, or the arts. Many continue to stay involved with the sport they have loved since childhood, coaching young children or volunteering with local school teams.

EARNINGS

Today, professional athletes who are members of top-level teams earn hundreds of thousands of dollars in prize money at professional competitions; the top players or athletes in each sport earn as much or more in endorsements and advertising, usually for sports-related products and services, but increasingly for products or services completely unrelated to their sport. Such salaries and other incomes are not representative of the whole field of professional athletes, but are only indicative of the fantastic revenues a few rare athletes with extraordinary talent can hope to earn. In 2003 athletes had median annual earnings of $45,780, according to the U.S. Department of Labor. Ten percent earned less than $13,310.

Perhaps the only caveat to the financial success of an elite athlete is the individual's character or personality. An athlete with a bad temper or prone to unsportsman-like behavior may still be able to participate in team play, helping to win games and garner trophies, but he or she won't necessarily be able to cash in on the commercial endorsements. Advertisers are notoriously fickle about the spokespeople they choose to endorse products; some athletes have lost million-dollar accounts because of their bad behavior on and off the court.

WORK ENVIRONMENT

Athletes compete in many different conditions, according to the setting of the sport (indoors or outdoors) and the rules of the organizing or governing bodies. Athletes who participate in football or soccer, for example, often compete in hot, rainy, or freezing conditions, but at any point, organizing officials can call off the match, or postpone competition until better weather.

Indoor events are less subject to cancellation. However, since it is in the best interests of an organization not to risk the athletes' health, any condition that might adversely affect the outcome of a competition is usually reason to cancel or postpone it. The coach or team physician, on the other hand, may withdraw an athlete from a game if he or she is injured or ill. Nerves and fear are not good reasons to default on a competition, and part of ascending into the ranks of professional athletes means learning to cope with the anxiety that comes with competition. Some athletes, however, actually thrive on the nervous tension.

In order to reach the elite level of any sport, athletes must begin their careers early. Most professional athletes have been honing their skills since they were quite young. Athletes fit hours of practice time into an already full day; many famous players practiced on their own in the hours before school, as well as for several hours after school during team practice. Competitions are often far from the young athlete's home, which means they must travel on a bus or in a van with the team and coaching staff. Sometimes young athletes are placed in special training programs far from their homes and parents. They live with other athletes training for the same sport or on the same team and only see their parents for holidays and vacations. The separation from a child's parents and family can be difficult; often an athlete's family decides to move to be closer to the child's training facility.

The expenses of a sport can be overwhelming, as is the time an athlete must devote to practice and travel to and from competitions. Although most high school athletic programs pay for many expenses, if the athlete wants additional training or private coaching, the child's parents must come up with the extra money. Sometimes young athletes can get official sponsors or they might qualify for an athletic scholarship from the training program. In addition to specialized equipment and clothing, the athlete must sometimes pay for a coach, travel expenses, competition fees and, depending on the sport, time at the facility or gym where he or she practices. Gymnasts, for example, train for years as individuals, and then compete for positions on national or international teams. Up until the time they are accepted (and usually during their participation in the team), these gymnasts must pay for their expenses—from coach to travel to uniforms to room and board away from home.

Even with the years of hard work, practice, and financial sacrifice that most athletes and their families must endure, there is no guarantee that an athlete will achieve the rarest of the rare in the sports world—financial reward. An athlete needs to truly love the sport at which he or she excels, and also have a nearly insatiable ambition and work ethic.

OUTLOOK

The outlook for professional athletes will vary depending on the sport, its popularity, and the number of positions open with professional teams. On the whole, the outlook for the field of professional sports is healthy, but the number of jobs will not increase dramatically. Some sports, however, may experience a rise in popularity, which will translate into greater opportunities for higher salaries, prize monies, and commercial endorsements.

TO LEARN MORE ABOUT PROFESSIONAL ATHLETES

BOOKS

Benson, Michael. *Hank Aaron: Baseball Player.* Ferguson Career Biographies. New York: Facts On File, 2005.

Christopher, Matt. *Great Moments in Baseball History.* New York: Little, Brown, 1996.

———. *On the Field with Derek Jeter.* New York: Little, Brown, 2000.

Freedman, Russell. *Babe Didrikson Zaharias.* New York: Clarion, 1999.

Krull, Kathleen. *Lives of the Athletes: Thrills, Spills (And What the Neighbors Thought).* New York: Harcourt Brace, 1997.

Rudeen, Kenneth. *Jackie Robinson.* New York: Harper-Trophy, 1996.

FOR MORE INFORMATION

Individuals interested in pursuing a career in a professional team sport should speak to their coach and contact the professional organization for that sport to receive further information. For other ideas on how to pursue a career in a professional team sport, contact

American Alliance for Health, Physical Education, Recreation, and Dance

1900 Association Drive

Reston, VA 20191-1598

Tel: 800-213-7193

http://www.aahperd.org

For a free brochure and information on the Junior Olympics and more, contact

Amateur Athletic Union

PO Box 22409

Lake Buena Vista, FL 32830

Tel: 407-934-7200

http://www.aausports.org

TO LEARN MORE ABOUT ROBERTO CLEMENTE

BOOKS

Bjarkman, Peter. *Baseball with a Latin Beat*. Jefferson, N.C.: McFarland, 1994.

Christine, Bill. *Numero Uno: Roberto*. New York: Stadia Sports, 1973.

Falkner, David. *Nine Sides of the Diamond: Baseball's Great Glove Men and the Fine Art of Defense*. New York: Simon & Schuster, 1990.

Hano, Arnold. *Roberto Clemente: Batting King*. New York: Putnam, 1968.

Markusen, Bruce. *Roberto Clemente: The Great One*. Champaign, Ill.: Sports Publishing, 1998.

Miller, Ira, and United Press International. *Roberto Clemente*. New York: Grosset & Dunlap, 1973.

Musick, Phil. *Reflections on Roberto*. Champaign, Ill.: Sports Publishing, 2001.

————. *Who Was Roberto?: A Biography of Roberto Clemente*. Garden City, N.Y.: Doubleday, 1974.

O'Brien, Jim. *Maz and the '60 Bucs: When Pittsburgh and Its Pirates Went All the Way*. Pittsburgh: Jim O'Brien Publishing, 1993.

————. *Remember Roberto: Clemente Recalled by Teammates, Family, Friends and Fans*. Pittsburgh: Jim O'Brien Publishing, 1994.

Wagenheim, Kal. *Clemente!* New York: Praeger, 1973.

MAGAZINES

Abrams, Al. "Clemente Better than Waner, Youngs?" *Baseball Digest*, May 1967.

Allen, Maury. "Final Look: Roberto Clemente." *Beckett Baseball Card Monthly*, September 1993.

Anderson, Dave. "Roberto Clemente's Spirit Lives On." *Baseball Digest*, June 1976.

Biederman, Les. "The Clemente Intrigue." *Baseball Digest*, July 1955.

Blass, Steve. "A Teammate Remembers Roberto Clemente." *Sport*, April 1973.

Caceres, M.I. "The Unforgettable Roberto Clemente." *Reader's Digest*, July 1973.

Chastain, Bill. "Right Field Rifle." *Sports History*, January 1989.

Clemente, Roberto. "The Game I'll Never Forget." *Baseball Digest*, September 1971.

———. "Clemente Left His Mark." *Baseball Research Journal*, 1973.

Cohn, Howard. "Roberto Clemente's Problem." *Sport*, May 1962.

Cope, Myron. "Aches and Pains and Three Batting Titles." *Sports Illustrated*, March 7, 1966.

Falls, Joe. "The General Managers Pick Baseball's Best Player." *Sport*, March 1968.

Feeney, Charley, "Clemente Next to Join 3000-Hit Club." *Baseball Digest*, October 1969.

Feldman, Jay. "Roberto Clemente Went to Bat for All Latino Ballplayers." *Smithsonian*, September 1993.

Green, Jerry. "Clemente's Plaint." *Baseball Digest*, August 1967.

Guilfoile, Bill, Joe Chadys, and Sally O'Leary, editors. *Pirates Yearbook '72: World Champion Pittsburgh Pirates*, 1972.

Heiling, Joe. "Roberto Clemente, the Pirates' Thoroughbred." *Baseball Digest*, January 1972.

Jordan, Pat. "Clemente and Oliva: Same Ends, Different Means." *Sport*, November 1970.

Kahn, Roger. "Golden Triumphs, Tarnished Dreams." *Sports Illustrated*, August 30, 1976.

Klein, Larry. "Clemente Keeps Them on Their Toes." *Sport*, October 1960.

———. "Manny Sanguillen Remembers Roberto." *Baseball Digest*, May 1973.

Mazeroski, Bill, with Phil Musick. "My 16 Years with Roberto Clemente." *Sport*, November 1971.

Murdock, Eugene. "Clemente Joins Exclusive Three-Crown Club." *Baseball Digest*, December 1965.

Peters, Jess. "Roberto Clemente: Mr. Pittsburgh Pirates." *Black Sports*, November 1972.

Peterson, Robert W. "The Pride of Puerto Rico." *Boy's Life*, November 1991.

Prato, Lou. "Why the Pirates Love the New Roberto Clemente." *Sport*, August 1967.

Richman, Milton. "Clemente was a Sensitive Super Star." *Baseball Digest*, March 1973.

Ripp, Bart. "A Fan Remembers Roberto Clemente." *Sport*, April 1973.

———. "Roberto Clemente." *Sports Illustrated*, September 19, 1994.

———. "Roberto Clemente, An Extraordinary Man." *Baseball Digest*, March 1972.

Ruck, Rob. "Remembering Roberto." *Pittsburgh*, December 1992.

Shecter, Leonard. "Clemente Did It the Hard Way." *Baseball Digest*, July 1962.

Smizik, Bob. "Roberto Clemente Would Have Been Proud of Memorial Statue." *Baseball Digest*, November 1994.

Vass, George. "Clemente: Baseball's Most Complete Player." *Baseball Digest*, May 1970.

———. "Viva Roberto." *Ebony*, September 1967.

Ways, C.R. "'Nobody Does Anything Better than Me in Baseball,' Says Roberto Clemente." *New York Times Magazine*, April 9, 1972.

Wolf, Bob. "The Strain of Being Roberto Clemente." *Life*, May 24, 1968.

Wulf, Steve. "Arriba Roberto." *Sports Illustrated*, December 29, 1992.

Zeske, Mark. "Mementos of Roberto." *Beckett Vintage Sports*, September 1997.

NEWSPAPERS

"Clemente, Pirates' Star, Dies in Crash of Plane Carrying Aid to Nicaragua." *The New York Times*, January 1, 1973.

Daley, Arthur. "In Tribute to Roberto Clemente." *The New York Times*, January 2, 1973.

Feeney, Charley. "Clemente Has His Night, Bucs Make It a Big One." *Pittsburgh Post-Gazette*, July 25, 1970, p. 1.

Newhan, Ross. "A Living, Loving Tribute to Roberto Clemente." *Los Angeles Times*, December 12, 1984.

Smith, Chester L. "Clemente Ranks with Paul Waner as Top Outfielder." *The Pittsburgh Press*, July 14, 1961.

VIDEOS

1971 World Series Highlight Video. Major League Baseball Productions, 1972.

Clemente. Black Canyon Productions (aired on Fox Sports), 1998.

Roberto: A Video Tribute. Major League Baseball Productions, 1993.

WEBSITES

Official Roberto Clemente Website

http://www.robertoclemente21.com

Baseball Hall of Fame

http://www.baseballhalloffame.org

Latino Sports Legends

http://www.latinosportslegends.com

INDEX

Page numbers in *italics* indicate illustrations.

ABOUT THE AUTHOR

Jerry Roberts is an author, critic, and freelance writer. His books include *The Eastern Cougar: Historical Accounts, Scientific Investigations, New Evidence; The Great American Playwrights on the Screen; Mitchum: In His Own Words; Robert Mitchum: A Bio-Bibliography; Rain Forest Bibliography;* and *Movie Talk From the Front Lines: Interviews with Filmmakers by the Los Angeles Film Critics Association.* He is a former columnist and critic for both the former Cinemania website and Copley Los Angeles Newspapers. He is a past vice president and secretary of the Los Angeles Film Critics Association. A former sports editor of several Pennsylvania newspapers, he also was a news reporter for the *Pittsburgh Post-Gazette.* His byline has appeared in *Daily Variety, Hollywood Reporter, DGA Magazine, Video Business, Films in Review, Editor & Publisher, Final Take,* and many other periodicals. He lives in California.